D0374394

Connecting
Creativity and Spirituality

Christian Koontz

Sheed & Ward

Dedication

to

Hagia Sophia
and the children of the world
who are Her joy,
especially Kristen Margaret
and Noelle

Sheed & Ward ™ is a service of National Catholic Reporter Publishing, Inc.

Library of Congress Catalog Card Number: 86-61360

ISBN: 0-934134-96-0

Published by: Sheed & Ward
        115 E. Armour Blvd. P.O. Box 414292
        Kansas City, MO 64141-0281

To order, call: (800) 821-7926

Contents

Foreword

This journal was written in midsummer, 1983, then put aside until a long-forgotten copy made its way to some unknown kindred spirits and was returned to me. Their response encouraged me to offer the journal to a wider audience. Preparing it for publication in spring, 1985, I saw it afresh as the chronicle of a brief and intense encounter between my inner self and my outer work.

Such encounters are part of a searching we are scarcely aware of, a searching for growing intimacy between our inner opus and our outer work. We do not initiate such a search; we are drawn into it by the very nature of life. Nor do we ever conclude the search; we are just drawn deeper and deeper into it until we discover that we are not the searcher but the searched. Then the action shifts radically: we surrender searching and allow ourselves to be searched.

Through a dialectical process of trial and error we gradually discover how and when to act to make the most of the givens of our life, our gifts, and limitations of nature and grace. In essence, it is truly loving knowing we seek, a knowing that grows more certain over time yet remains always veiled and obscure. It is Hagia Sophia we seek.

Preface

Late last night I put the finishing touches on you, *Connecting*. Oppressive heat and a lightning storm blocked the entrance to sleep. Listening to the thunder, I wondered how to introduce you properly to others. Soon I also found myself surprised by the appearance of a germ of an idea and plans for your next sibling.

Smiling, I recalled your words about the courage it takes to complete an artwork: every ending is also a beginning of a new challenge. The process never stops until we surrender life. In the coming months I will try to give life to your brother. You have taught me much about how to do that more tenderly. I will try to be faithful to that teaching.

In the meanwhile, you make your own way alone now, "a hostage to fortune." Go in peace. You really do not need an introduction. You are what you are – no more, no less. Simply be yourself. You can speak your own word now, in your own way. I hope you will meet a few friends among those who keep watch in the night. If so, I know you will keep watch with them.

1.   The Story

I remain puzzled. I came to Notre Dame this summer to take a two-week course on spirituality and to do some private research. The course, a rich and challenging experience, just ended. The materials for the other research that I thought were here are not here. I have nineteen days relatively free of responsibilities. Should I leave Notre Dame now or should I stay? I do not know. Just what am I to do next? I do not know.

I must wait and see. While waiting, I will relax, rest, and make contact with friends. I will enjoy myself, trusting that what I want and need to do next will be made clear to me in good time.

An idea: perhaps I should use these nineteen days to attempt yet again writing the book on creativity and spirituality that has been struggling to be born in me for three years?

A familiar voice objects, "But you can't do that. You do not have your materials with you. A few relevant books, maybe, but none of the voluminous notes and pages and pages of aborted attempts that have accumulated since the germ of the book first appeared."

"That is all right," a deeper voice responds. "Risk it. See where it goes. Presumptuous? Perhaps. If so, that will be made clear to you in due time. 'Fare forward,' as Eliot says."

Yes, fare forward. This present period of fresh ideas from the course and puzzlement over what to do next may well be part of the process: learning when to work and when to let go of working and simply waiting. When we let go of trying, often the insight we need to take us forward is given to us, at a time, in a place, and through means often quite unexpected. So I begin to write.

Let it be said at the outset that I write this book because I need to write it and I want to write it. Creativity keeps me alive. Through writing, I can become more conscious of the creative process as it works in me and through me. Then perhaps I can praise it more fitly, rejoice in it more heartily, and enter into it more responsibly. In other words, through writing perhaps I can have more abundant life.

If you, my reader, share my need and desire, then this book may be for you. Otherwise, reading it may be a waste of your time and energy. If you share my need and desire, however, perhaps sharing my explorations and discoveries will interest you and encourage you in living your own life more creatively. If so, I would be most grateful. You are, after all, my sister or brother, created like me to be a creator in your own right, in your own way, and in your own time. If you do not share my interest, that is all right, too, of course.

An experience comes immediately to mind, an experience that marked a turning point in my own adventures with creativity. First, some background.

In the late 1960's I had been a doctoral student studying medieval literature, literary criticism, and linguistics at a major Catholic university. When I finished my studies in 1970, I returned to teach English at a small Catholic college in northwestern Pennsylvania. One of the courses I taught was creative writing. Another was a course analyzing the rhetoric of revolution. I did not know then the profound connection between the two.

During the course in creative writing, I worked with a young man who was experimenting with drugs. He spoke rather freely of writing under the influence of LSD, believing that this helped him to be more creative. While I did not really understand this and was a little uneasy with it, I tried to be open and noncondemning.

At the end of the course I asked the class to evaluate what we had done together. This young man – I will call him BJ – criticized me for not paying enough attention to the role of the unconscious in writing. I did not really understand this criticism, but it struck a deep chord of truth in me.

From that time on, about 1971, I began to pay attention to what BJ had said. For me that meant reading about the unconscious, especially in the work of Carl Jung. After some time, I began also to pay closer and closer attention to the unconscious processes that underlay my own writing and that of my students and professional writers.

Gradually, this reflection and reading began to balance each other and establish steadier, rhythmic cycles of experience, reflection, and study. I see now the influence of my Western, masculine-oriented, academic training: start with the authorities – the authors – rather than with the Author who speaks to us most eloquently in and through our experience of living.

By the late 70's I had begun to sense a crucial connection between creativity in the arts, sciences, and philosophy and creativity in spirituality. Although I lacked a sufficiently profound grasp of the fundamental nature of either realm of the creative, I gradually became more and more aware of the integral connection. And so I was off on another journey: to seek those connections and articulate them.

By 1981 I was teaching not only creative writing, but also a more general course in creativity at another small Catholic college in Michigan. In that course I began to work through some of the connections that I had discovered. As is always the case, I learned a great deal from my students. Their interest and encouragement further motivated me to continue trying to articulate my experience and understanding in writing.

Questions and Challenge

That brings me to the present moment, yet another attempt to articulate the principal questions that have arisen and to hazard some answers to these questions:

- Why is creativity such a compelling, even urgent, issue for me?
- What is creativity?
- What is its basis?
- What is its purpose?
- How can I become more creative?
- How can I help others become more creative?
- What inhibits creativity?
- What fosters creativity?
- What is spirituality?
- What is the link between creativity and spirituality?
- What are their differences?

- Do these questions matter?
- If so, why?
- Who cares?

My questions arose in roughly the order above, but the last one is probably the first to be addressed: who cares? From most of the evidence, few of us could care less.

A Problem Misconceived

But God cares. God really cares because that is precisely why God created us in the first place: that we might be, in turn, creators. In our ignorance and illusion, we too easily forget this fact. Little wonder we do. Our philosophies and systems of education too often squelch it early in life. Our attempts at something new often result in misunderstanding, discouragement, and failure. Why bother? Who cares?

By virtue of our very creation, we each have within us the divine energy and sense of direction we need to co-operate with God in creating ourselves and in adding to the richness, diversity, and beauty of the universe. If we could but believe this truth and act upon it, the kingdom of peace and love would become a reality even in our time.

An Unexpected Encounter

Later the same day, July 2. A knock on the door of my room here in the dormitory interrupts my writing this morning. I answer it. Before my puzzled sight stands a woman I had seen around campus but did not know.

Another woman quickly steps into view. It is a young woman, formerly a member of my own congregation and now with another. I express my delight at seeing her. Immediately, I notice her serenity and fitness. She is brown from the sun and comfortably dressed in a red T-shirt and khaki shorts. I invite them in. We talk, sharing news of ourselves and mutual friends and acquaintances.

As we talk, I am aware that the young woman is an embodiment of all I have been writing about. She is a religious woman and a gifted musician, able to compose and perform and teach music. She looks well and happy. I sense that she is her own person. Such a surprise that she should come by to say hello at this particular time . . . But not really. The creative God is above all a God of surprises, manifesting power and presence when and where and in whatever form it pleases. So we should not be surprised when we are surprised – but grateful.

A Crucial Visitation

Later I walk to a retreat house at the edge of campus to meet a recent acquaintance. While we have met elsewhere only twice, we seemed to have much in common. Now seems a good time for a visit.

We talk, sitting in the shade on a grassy rise. Soon I hear myself sharing with her my puzzlement at not knowing just what I am to do now that my course is over. I tell her of my morning sense that I should use this unexpected time to write my book on creativity and spirituality. I feel sure that this book should be written and that I should write it, but I have not been able to do so. I express my frustration.

My friend suggests that perhaps I lack the courage to "put it out there." I reject that notion. No, I do not think that is true. I have just finished writing a book on the teaching of writing and offered it for publication. It has been rejected by one major publishing house, but another asked to see it, so I sent it off to them and await their response in peace. No, I am not really afraid. Fear may come fleetingly, but it does not deflect me from my work. No, it must be something else, but I cannot put my finger on it.

Another insight from my friend. Perhaps the problem is not with the *contents* of the book but with the *form*? Perhaps I need to risk the form as well as the ideas?

This suggestion touches toward the center. Does the nature of my topic, creativity, militate against the scholarly, systematic, analytical method and form I have been attempting for years? By its very nature, would creativity resist being confined to such a method and form?

That strikes me as possibly true, if not in general, at least for me. Yet I do not think that I am afraid of risking the form, either. Something else is operating here, but I still do not know what it is.

We continue talking, and clarity continues to happen, drawing me closer to the center of my friend's insight. I see the necessary distinction. I am not afraid of *risking* the form. The problem is rather that I do not *know* what the appropriate form *is*. In this instance it is ignorance, not cowardice, that seems to be inhibiting me.

The Emergence of a Purpose

Connection: let the appropriate form arise as it will, just

as the ideas to be in-formed have arisen. Then go with it wherever it takes me. I recall Theodore Roethke's "I wake to sleep and take my waking slow./ I learn by going where I have to go."

Instead of going on a head trip and just talking *about* creativity, treating it merely intellectually, perhaps I need to let both the method and the form of this book-to-be emerge as they will. Then the completed work might reflect, however obscurely, something of the process of its coming to be, and it might also embody the very insights that I have been trying to express.

Connection: now I know my real purpose in writing this book is to mirror and embody the creative process rather than simply to talk about it.

So that was the crux of the problem. I had assumed what the method and form should be. "To assume," a teacher once said, "is to make an ass out of you and an ass out of me." So I had not been open to a method and form appropriate to the very nature of my subject. I had unconsciously been trying to force on my topic an inappropriate method and form that I have been schooled to and become comfortable with: the systematic development of a logical argument on an issue. Following a masculine method, I had been trying to write a book that must follow a feminine method.

Had it been written, that book would have lacked integrity. Would I have been false in writing it, since the feminine spirit in me is stronger than the masculine mind? Such a book never existed in the mind of God, and I was never meant to write it. However much I tried to make it become what I thought it should be, we both resisted. A sobering thought . . . As Ira Progoff says, "What if you succeed at the wrong thing?" A sobering question . . .

I had violated the very nature of what I wanted to communicate, the nature and workings of the creative process
in us. The form itself is part of the meaning. Instead of allowing the appropriate form – the natural form – to
emerge organically along with the ideas, I myself had determined, however unconsciously, just what that form
should be. Not deliberately, so no guilt. Nonetheless, I had
made that decision. I had been untrue to the process, trying to force my ideas into a predetermined gridwork. Hap-
pily, if frustratingly, the work seems to be stronger than I,
and it would not cooperate in my oppression of it.

Further realization: I had violated the nature of the
process in yet another way. Since I had not *asked* for the
method and form to be given me, I was not open to receiving it. "Ask and you shall receive. Knock and it shall be
opened to you." As Flannery O'Connor says, "I write what
I am given." I might add, "I must ask for what I am to
write." God – not we – always takes the initiative in
genuine creativity. I had thus assumed an initiative not
mine to assume. I had been irresponsible.

Walking back to the dorm, I acknowledge and accept
these violations of the nature of the creative process. I
ask to be given the method and form that this work long-
aborning needs and wants to take, if it is to be the book
it is meant to be and do the work it is meant to do.

As I walk and ponder, I hear the bells of Sacred Heart
Church announcing that Saturday afternoon mass would
soon begin. I decide to attend. As I try to be present to
what is taking place, more ideas about the method and
form of the book begin to flow: start with *experiences* that
brought me insights into the nature and workings of

creativity. Then *reflect* on those experiences and articulate the results of my reflections. (My teacher had taught me well. Experience is the principal locus of God's revelation.) And so the corpus of my thought will take the form natural to it?

Perhaps, then, the book should be a journal of this present experience of allowing a book to be born? This strikes me right, and I determine to go with it as far as it will take me. A connection has been made, thank God and Christian. We are moving forward together, this embryo book and I. "But right now," an inner voice interrupts, "you are at mass. So be here now. Time enough for all these thoughts later."

Method and Attitude

Later. Connections: a key moment in the creative process. When we are creating, we are allowing connections to happen – allowing connections to be made in the arts, allowing connections to be seen in philosophy and science, allowing connections to be done in morality, allowing connections to be experienced in religious experience, and allowing connections to be lived in spirituality. The materials and the operations may differ, but creativity always involves bringing something new into being through connecting.

So this book should be called *Connecting: Creativity and Spirituality*. That sounds good. Not *connections*, but *connecting*. A verbal form, to better convey the dynamism of the process. Let it be so for now.

Another idea: Should I write this book, at least in part, on the word processor, thereby redeeming in some small

way that machine that can be used for destructive purposes? Yes.

Confirmation of an earlier idea: try to keep the book
anecdotal, drawing on concrete experience. That will help
prevent me from escaping into generalities and abstrac-
tions, keep me rooted in reality. "What is good is always
concrete," says Lonergan. Our real growth as persons is
in the direction of "greater concreteness on the part of
the subject."

The journal method will assist that concreteness. In
fact, it strikes me that the journal form has been trying to
reveal itself to me for a long time, because I have written
many journal entries on this topic over the years. Just this
morning when I started to write, I naturally did so in a
journal entry. Yet I did not make the connection until I
was open to receiving it.

A variety of journal techniques should help: dialogues,
listings, imaging, mantras. Be open to them all, as the
spirit moves. And to any other techniques or forms that
present themselves to me.

Beneath the techniques maintain a contemplative at-
titude. In one sense, contemplation is useless; it has no
practical value. We enter into contemplation not for what
we can get out of it, but for what we can bring to it – ourselves. We try to be present to God Who is always present
to us, though we are seldom aware of God's presence. We
go to meet God where God is most at home, deep within
our own hearts. As a wise woman put it so poignantly,
"God is deeply down . . . deeply down."

We do not do anything down there. We just sit as close
as we can get to God. We simply make ourselves available
for God's self-revelation to us, if God chooses to give us

that revelation. If it happens, it happens, and we enjoy God's company for awhile – or we squirm. If it doesn't happen, that is all right, too. God is free, after all, to do as God likes. And so are we.

A paradox of contemplation is that the more useless we allow ourselves to be, the more we find ourselves in the seed-bed of genuine creativity. Just being there, inert as a seed, our roots are drawn deeper into the heart of creativity. Sooner or later, the sap of life begins to flow through those roots toward the surface. Eventually a new creation – a new artwork, a new idea, a new action, a new relationship, or a new person – breaks through the underground darkness into the light of day. By doing nothing, we have unleashed "the force that through the green fuse drives the flower," to borrow a line from Dylan Thomas.

We learn the meaning of these lines only slowly over a lifetime of discovering that truly happy and fruitful experiences flow from initiatives not our own. We do not deliberately think them up or manufacture them. They come when we respond to spontaneous impulses from deep within us or to requests or invitations from others. Or they often come out of circumstances in which we find ourselves. We discover that if we really want to respond to these invitations and we can do so freely and simply, then we are truly joyful. This joy is deeper than the surface satisfaction and superficial pleasure we so often settle for.

We learn it also through opposite experiences. When we act on initiatives that do not come from our depths but from our surface selves, or when we presume to do things for others that they do not really ask us to do, we are dissatisfied and uneasy. When we do things that we do not really want to do or that we are not really able to do freely and simply, we are sad and unproductive.

Any valid theory of creativity must begin here: God always takes the initiative. In quite concrete situations, God issues the invitation through a spontaneous, inner impulse, through another's request or invitation, or through some external circumstance.

The first initiative God took was to create us in the divine image and likeness. We are created, and we are created precisely to be creators. This truth is so stunning that we can't seem to absorb it. It knocks us out of our senses – senseless, in more ways than one. It is not a pipe dream. It is real. It is true.

We must return again and again to ponder this astounding truth, and more importantly, begin to live it, before it begins to become real for us. The more we live out of this truth, the more real it becomes for us. Then one day, the light begins to dawn on us that we do not simply think it to be true or believe it to be true, we know it to be true because we have experienced its truth for ourselves.

Like God, we have our deepest meaning and truest fulfillment in creating and enjoying creation. Apart from creating and enjoying creation, we feel ugly, unfulfilled, meaningless, and alienated from ourselves and from our world. And well we might feel this way, because we are this way in fact.

Feeling our meaninglessness and alienation is a gift, a gift being offered in great abundance in our time, an age of alienation. When we allow ourselves really to feel this alienation, the dissonance within us begins to generate the energy and search for direction that can fulfill our need for connectedness, fulfillment, and beauty. Such dissonance is God acting in our lives. It is God taking the initiative to generate the energy we need for creative living and for creating authentic artworks.

Another connection: this is why I feel such longing and urgency to create. I was made to do so, meant to do so, from the beginning of time and perhaps before. And so were you.

And the ultimate purpose of it all? To embody the love that issues forth in life beautiful to contemplate:

> God found it very good.
> *Genesis* 1:31

Creativity and the Breath of Life

Another connection: This is why it is crucial that I tell this story, as best I can, to share with others what I have been offered and, however imperfectly, accepted. I am most alive when I am most creative. I am sick when I refuse to be creative.

So is my world sick when it refuses to be creative. Nuclear proliferation, wars, crime, torture, poverty, manipulation, and oppression of all sorts are the fruits of our corporate refusal to create and our corporate refusal to allow and enable others to create. Such refusal robs all of us and our world of our birthright and prevents God from doing as God wants: creating the world and enjoying it.

We have two basic choices in life. We may create or destroy. Whichever we choose, we will bear the consequences. "By their fruits you shall know them." Together we are making history and what may well be the end of history with the fruits of our refusal to create. So many fruits of our Age of Destruction are blighted, misshapen, and rotten to the core. How God must mourn over what we have done to the Garden of Eden through the abuse of our freedom and imagination! Well might we, too, mourn. Let us put an end to mourning and do something about it.

But how turn aside from choosing destruction? How turn back toward choosing creation? I am led again to *Genesis*, but this time to the second story of creation told there.

> The Lord God formed a human out of the clay of the ground and blew into that human's nostrils the breath of life, and so the human became a living being.
>
> *Genesis* 2:7

The secret of life and creativity is the breath of God breathing through us. Entering into this breath, breathing it and allowing it to breathe us, we have life. And here springs a second insight into the Age of Destruction: We are stifling this breath, the very breath of God that breathes all things into being. The world is running out of breath. Our world is dying.

A memory arises. I sit beside an elderly man, brown and thin and graying, at a Sander's lunch counter in northwest Detroit, having breakfast. Many old folks in my deteriorating neighborhood come here for an inexpensive meal and some companionship. I sometimes join them to eat, watch, listen, and talk. My neighbor begins to talk. I do not remember most of what he said, but I do remember enjoying his wisdom. In the midst of it all, he said that the secret of long life – so his grandfather told him – is to "just keep breathing." I laughed, and dimly recognized the profound truth of what he had said.

2. Letting It Happen

July 3, 10:30 a.m. I awoke this morning with thoughts streaming, as they sometimes do upon awaking. Sleep cleanses our heart and mind, allowing our spirit to flow more freely. Having the time, the need, and the desire, this time I let it flow.

Realization: one thing leads naturally to another. That is the creative process at its best. It is really so simple, but we have complicated it out of all semblance to reality. Way leads on to way – if we but let it. I think of Dorothy Day's long loneliness – so fertile, blossoming in good news for the poor, good news for all of us.

We were just sitting there talking when Peter Maurin came in.

We were just sitting there talking when lines of people began to form, saying "We need bread." We could not say, "Go, be thou filled." If there were six loaves and a few fishes, we had to divide them. There was always bread.

We were just sitting there talking and people moved in on us. Let those who can take it, take it. Some moved out and that made room for more. And somehow the walls expanded.

17

> We were just sitting there talking and some-
> one said, "Let's all go live on a farm."
>
> It was as casual as all that, I often think. It
> just came about. It just happened.
>
> I found myself, a barren woman, the joyful
> mother of children. It is not always easy to be
> joyful, to keep in mind the duty of delight . . .
>
> It all happened while we sat there talking, and
> it is still going on.
> > *The Long Loneliness*, pp. 285-286.

Yes, the creative process at its truest is just that casual
– no big deal. And it is still going on, in you and in me, in
all of us, if we but let it. Our hardest work in creativity,
perhaps, is to be ourselves and let the rest of reality be
what it is. Let it be. Let it be, and it will naturally be creative. So easy, but we make it so hard.

My listening upon waking tells me also that yesterday's
insight into the probable method and form of this book was
probably valid: let this book of connections spin itself out
as it will, in journal form. I am writing now more easily
and freely than usual. It feels right. It makes sense to me.
After all my work and study in journal writing, it has become natural to me.

Feminine Spirit and Masculine Mind

The method then is not to begin with the deductive, an-
alytic, and systematic, but rather with the inductive, in-

tuitive, associative, and organic. Do not follow syllogistic method, the method developed over centuries through the predominance of the masculine mind. That mind has been insufficiently corrected by the associative and intuitive methods of feminine spirit. As a result, we have distorted the creative process, falsified it at its very roots, and truncated it. That is why we are where we are, as individual persons, as a nation, and as a world: a distorted, falsified, and truncated people. No wonder the world – and we – groan in agony.

But not to worry. That is also why we are where we are with the growing recognition of the value of the feminine spirit in both women and men. The recovery of the feminine spirit is now being painfully effected everywhere. This recovery of the feminine in all of us is crucial to the survival of the planet. Let the feminine spirit take its rightful place, in creative tension with the masculine mind.

It therefore seems appropriate that a woman writing about creativity would let the writing flow as it will. But not chaotically, irrationally. The creative process is a natural, nonrational process, but it must be rationally controlled. We have to keep our wits about us when we create. In writing, this means following some logical pattern so that our thoughts will be accessible to minds other than our own.

Logic builds a bridge between two minds. The writer builds the bridge so that she might cross over it to meet her reader. Once over the bridge, the writer can share her thoughts and help the reader bring to consciousness what she thinks or feels or senses or believes or knows. Logic helps us communicate, become one.

Logic is necessary, then, but logic cannot provide the materials for the bridge. Experience, reflection, and intuition do that. And the logic need not be that of the syllogism – the logic so slowly and necessarily forged over centuries out of the seminal thought of those glorious Greek thinkers, especially Aristotle. There are, after all, other logics. The Greek thinkers knew of them, too. Plato spoke sometimes, for example, of the organic nature of creativity. Yet they and their male successors in the western world chose to emphasize the technical component of creativity, the conscious effort that organizes things logically and revises and refines that order.

That effort has done its work – and more than its proper work. It needs now to be balanced with due attention to unconscious inspiration, the mysterious and nonsyllogistic, that generates the material to be crafted. So let this book be a marriage of inspiration and logic; let the feminine and masculine be wed in it, with the feminine taking the lead and the masculine following, for a change. Let it be something new and different.

Losing Touch With The Source

Later: I see that, exploring the first layer of thoughts given me, I have gone quite a way since yesterday. But back now, circle back to the beginning of this book and the beginning of the human story. After talking with my friend yesterday, I began to see other connections. Let them spin themselves out now.

The serpent's temptation of Eve: eat of the fruit and your eyes will be opened and you will be like gods who know what is good and what is bad.

So she took some of its fruit and ate it. Then the
eyes of both of them were opened, and they
realized that they were naked.
                    Genesis 3:1-7

The story, we must remember, is told by a man, from a
man's point of view. The man blames the woman. The
more likely truth is that both were responsible. Wanting
to see like gods, wanting to decide for themselves between
good and evil, together they distort the creative process
from the very beginning. Indeed the apple is rotten at the
core, and both of them eat of it.

Cast out of Eden, they must struggle with the other animals for survival. Because man is stronger in the gifts required for physical survival, he dominates. He can better
hunt other animals and do the back-breaking work of til-
ling the soil for food. He can hew out suitable places for
shelter and skin animals for clothing. He is also more fit
for physical combat with other men who threaten his life.
He is better, too, at the process of making the logical decisions required for physical survival.

Meanwhile, in the cave, woman is busy bearing and caring for their children. Because she is stronger of heart, she
nurtures the man and cares for him when he is sick and
wounded. Because she has an eye for beauty, she makes
their cave into a pleasant place to live. So they make their
way as best they can, living and working together: the
physically stronger man dominating and the physically
weaker woman cooperating in that domination. Together
they sink deeper into the gradual process of deciding for
themselves what is good for them and what is bad.

Over centuries, they gradually grow more and more out

of touch with the wellspring of life, the creative power that brought the world into being and the creative presence that sustains it. They lose touch with the wisdom that creates a discerning heart, a thinking heart able to make the spontaneous, more authentic decisions required for spiritual survival. They lose touch with the creative spirit that refuses to make judgments of good and bad based solely on the appearances of things. They lose touch with the spirit that witholds judgment until all the relevant facts are in, including the truths of intuition and feelings. They become alienated from the spirit that does not rush to a judgment based solely on reason, but which allows all of reality to reveal what is good and what is bad for them, in its own way and time.

Another connection: timing. But that must wait until later. Time now to go back and reread all that I have written, type it up on the word processor, then revise and refine it to make my meaning clearer and more precise. Time now for masculine mind to do its proper work. If feminine spirit has done its work well, then there should be something to work with. We shall see.

Brainstreaming

July 4, the beginning of the third day's work on this book. The work of the first two days was about equally divided between focused brainstreaming, and revising and editing on the word processor. Taking up my work this morning, I do not quite know where or how to begin – still feeling my way along, one step at a time.

There were no relevant ideas upon waking that I particularly want to explore just now. Perhaps begin where

I left off yesterday, with the issue of timing? Perhaps with reflection on this morning's meditation on Jesus as the way, the truth , and the life? Certainly either of these would be fruitful.

I sense, rather, it would be more appropriate now to talk of brainstreaming, having introduced the term above. *Brainstreaming*: a new word that brings together for me *brainstorming* and *stream-of-consciousness*. Yes, begin today's explorations here, because the creative process in action best begins with some form of brainstreaming. A little background may help to establish the importance of brainstreaming in the creative process.

Use of the stream-of-consciousness technique in the novel has been a major development of narrative fiction in the twentieth century. Some of the most creative modern novelists, such as Henry James, James Joyce, Virginia Woolf, and William Faulkner, experimented with stream-of-consciousness as a way of more fully delineating character and action.

The main tributary of narrative fiction up to the nineteenth century had been chronological, telling a story following the order of how events transpired in time. This made sense on one level of reality, the surface level: tell a story just as it happened, event by event.

In the epic period, as in ancient Greece and Anglo-Saxon England, poets sang from memory the wondrous deeds of a national hero who was bigger than life, such as Odysseus and Beowulf. In the Middle Ages the spell of Camelot was cast over the epic tales. Launcelot and Gawain and Troilus not only fought battles; they also fell in love. With the romanticization of the hero, the epic gave way to the romance as a major narrative form. By the nineteenth century, with the rise of modern science and the middle class, reality began to set in more deeply in fiction. The romance gave way to the realistic novel. With emphasis being placed on the concrete delineation of details of character and setting, as in Balzac's novels, stories became more realistic on the surface level. By the beginning of the twentieth century, realism had become the distinguishing characteristic of the modern novel.

But for the most part it was a surface realism. With the beginnings of depth psychology in the twentieth century, writers such as Henry James, brother of William James, the psychologist, turned their attention from surface realism to depth realism. They began to explore the possibilities of telling a story through the inner consciousness of their characters.

Our consciousness is characterized by a constant stream of sensations, images, thoughts, memories, and feelings. Realistic stories need no longer follow a chronological order. Our minds follow an associative order. One idea or feeling stimulates an association, and that in turn leads to another and another. And so was born stream-of-consciousness as a major technique in modern fiction

Stream-of-consciousness penetrates the surface of reality. In literature, it parallels the development simultaneously taking place in modern science. Modern science has discovered that physical objects are not really solid, only apparently so. In fact, physical objects are composed of a "sea of molecules" in constant motion. With this discovery modern thought deepened from a naive realism that sees only the surface of things to a critical realism that also sees beneath the surface.

Just as physical objects are in constant motion, so are spiritual beings. The depths of a human being are like a stream constantly in motion. This stream includes within it symbols that are rich in meaning and power. Emotion evokes symbols, and symbols, in turn, evoke emotion. These symbols have power to heal and direct and move us.

With the recognition of this depth dimension, the real and the symbolic came together in literature. It was a creative moment in modern fiction.

Another creative moment in modern times was the conscious development of brainstorming as a way of creative problem-solving. Brainstorming is a simple technique available to any person or group faced with a problem. One simply relaxes and allows all ideas and associations to come to the surface, however outlandish or impossible of realization they may be. Every idea is accepted and noted without comment, without criticism, and without judgment.

When the flow of ideas ceases, each is critically evaluated, and the best are adopted, developed, and refined. Such an approach has been made popular by Alex Osborne and others and is widely used today by creative persons in business, industry, and education.

Stream-of-consciousness in the modern novel and brainstorming as a creative approach to problem-solving draw upon the insights of modern depth psychology. The term *brainstreaming* brings together the telling of a story, stream-of-consciousness, and brainstorming. It provides us with access to the depths beneath the surface of our minds. It makes available to us both the symbolic and the real.

When we brainstream, we scoop up, so to speak, something of the continuous stream of our inner life. That rich matrix contains not only the best *ideas* we have for solving a problem, resolving an issue, or living comfortably with the ambiguity and mystery that are so much a part of living, but also the significant *feelings* that accompany the problem, issue, ambiguity, or mystery. We need to know not only what we think about something, but also how we feel about it, if we are to make the significant connections and authentic choices our artworks require.

Some Uses of Brainstreaming

Brainstreaming is most obviously helpful for writers. We can see this with Henry James. James was not only a superior novelist but also a literary theorist. He not only wrote novels, he was also conscious of how he wrote them. In his notebooks, he recorded and reflected on the creative process that brought his novels into being. These notebooks are a collection of his brainstreaming. In them we can trace the story of the organic growth of a novel such as *What Maisie Knew* from the mere germ of an idea, through the rough development of character and plot, to the polished gem of a finished novel.

Artists other than novelists have used brainstreaming to help them create their works. Teresa of Avila, that great artist in living religiously, for example, tells us the story of her life in the book she so appropriately called *The Book of the Mercies of God.* Beginning with early memories, she wrote the book without pause or divisions, allowing the words to pour freely through her pen.

By the time she wrote the book at the age of 50, Teresa had attained a remarkable degree of personality integration. Therefore the book is not, as it might appear, a mere jumble of impressions loosely connected by a chronological narrative. Rather, it is, as two contemporary editors describe it, "a remarkable unity."

Teresa's book is a literary achievement of high order. More than that, however, it is the concrete reflection of a human artwork in the making: the person who was Teresa of Avila. No doubt the writing of the book deepened and expanded that living artwork by bringing to Teresa's consciousness the process by which God and person cooperate in the making of this most magnificent of all artworks, a genuine human being, an "immortal diamond," embodying and reflecting the nature of God.

Not only literary artists, mystics, and saints, however, have found brainstreaming helpful in stimulating their creativity. So, too, have many philosophers, scientists, and ordinary persons. People of all times, cultures, and walks of life have used some form of brainstreaming to spin out the ideas and feelings they would later revise and refine into systematic essays and treatises, symphonies, paintings, dances, moral actions, and human relationships.

Because words are a primary material produced by the human brain, much brainstreaming naturally takes written form. But it need not. Primitive persons past and present, with highly developed memories and intimacy with their unconscious depths, brainstream orally or even silently. Such persons have constant and almost immediate access to their creative depths.

Drawing, too, can be a way of brainstreaming. Children who cannot read or write can express their inner selves in paint or clay or wood. Some persons in therapy find it helpful to draw whatever they think or feel, thus removing blocks to their creativity.

Some famous examples of drawing as brainstreaming are the notebooks of Leonardo da Vinci. In the pages of those notebooks da Vinci sketched freely the broad outlines and details of his paintings and inventions. Looking at them now, we can get a glimpse of that elusive, creative process as it flowed through da Vinci's heart and mind.

What can we learn from all this – those of us who are not creative geniuses? While we may not be able to match the geniuses' achievements in painting, or literature, or music, we may be able to match and even surpass their achievements in life process. We may be able to create a human artwork of equal or even greater stature than they attained. Whether greater or lesser, however, does not really matter. What matters is that we do the best we can to create the finest artwork made possible by our gifts, opportunities, and limitations.

We can learn from these geniuses to do as they did: brainstream and then revise and refine the material generated so that it can live on and enrich the world beyond the creator. We can do this as Teresa did, to help us in cooperating with God in the making of an artwork of our own life – the one artwork enjoined upon each of us through our creation and existence as an image and likeness of God.

Today spiritual journals, records of brainstreaming, are becoming more and more widely used. This is, I believe, another sign of hope that creativity is rising out of the ashes of our times. Along with the growing global consciousness and acceptance of the feminine spirit, this is a dramatic sign of the presence of the Spirit of Wisdom working in our world. In the process of such journalling, persons are allowing themselves to be transformed into a new creation.

A principal cause and outcome of such personal transformation is discernment of spirits. Discernment of spirits enables us to become more conscious of both the feelings and thoughts that lead us to make the decisions we make. Such discernment helps us to make more authentic decisions – decisions that flow from the true self rather than from the false self. Such authentic decisions, in turn, help retard the forces of destruction and liberate the forces of creativity within ourselves and within our world. If we are to make our way successfully through the modern confusion of values, discernment of spirits must come to complement the process of making merely logical decisions.

Books such as *The New Diary* contain many helpful ideas for working in such a journal. Ira Progoff's *Intensive Journal*® method, articulated in the book *At a Journal Workshop* and offered in workshops on an international scale, is perhaps the most systematic and fully developed approach to journal brainstreaming.

But we need not confine ourselves to brainstreaming through the written word or drawing. We can brainstream with tones and pitch in music, freely playing out the music within us. Or we can brainstream with movement, freely dancing out the contents of our minds and hearts. In whatever form it is expressed – spoken, written, drawn, played, or danced – brainstreaming can give us access to the creativity within us and let it flow forth to recreate and transform us and our world.

Brainstreaming is a godlike activity. The first story of

creation would give us the impression that God went about the creation of the world in a systematic, orderly fashion. But the second story of creation told in *Genesis* gives us a clue that that is only half the story. The other half is the truth that God *breathes* in us.

Wisdom and Creativity

This breath of God, the Spirit of Wisdom, breathes life into all things. And life is organic. It is not imposed from without; it grows from within. As Rosemary Haughton develops in an unpublished paper, "There is Hope for a Tree," many passages of the Wisdom books of the Old Testament complement the telling of the story of creation in *Genesis*. Such passages reveal the forgotten feminine side of the story, the role of the Spirit of Wisdom in creativity. They include *Proverbs* 8:22-29; *Sirach* 24; and this one from *Wisdom* 7: 21-29:

> Such things as are hidden I learned,
>   and such as are plain;
>   for Wisdom, the artificer of all,
>   taught me.
> For in her is a spirit
>   intelligent, holy, unique,
> Manifold, subtle, agile,
>   clear, unstained, certain,
> Not baneful, loving the good, keen,
>   unhampered, beneficent, kindly,
> Firm, secure, tranquil,
>   all-powerful, all-seeing,
> And pervading all spirits,
>   though they be intelligent, pure

and very subtle.
For Wisdom is mobile beyond all motion.
  and she penetrates and pervades all things
    by reason of her purity.
For she is an aura of the might of God
  and a pure effusion of the glory of the
    Almighty;
    therefore nought that is sullied enters into her.
For she is the refulgence of eternal light,
  the spotless mirror of the power of God,
  the image of his Goodness.
And she, who is one, can do all things,
  and renews everything while herself perduring;
And passing into holy souls from age to age,
  she produces friends of God and prophets.
For there is nought God loves, be it not
  one who dwells with Wisdom.
For she is fairer than the sun
  and surpasses every constellation of the stars.
Compared to light, she takes precedence;
  for that, indeed, night supplants,
  but wickedness prevails not over Wisdom.

Seeking a Pattern

Later: three days of brainstreaming, revising, and editing. Let me see if any pattern is emerging out of the chaos:

Day 1:
- Puzzlement over what to do next

- Experiences that led to the suggestion to write this book now

- Reason for writing

- Crucial experience with BJ that alerted me to the role of the unconscious in writing

- Study and reflection on the unconscious

- Connection between creativity and spirituality

- Encouragement to write a book on creativity

- Questions to be addressed in such a book

- Address to first question: who cares?

- Experience with a friend embodying creativity

- Discussion with another friend leading to insights on the causes of my blocks

- Asking for direction

- Appearance of journal method and form as appropriate

- *Connecting: Creativity and Spirituality*

- Use of word processor

- God as the initiator of all creativity

- First story of creation in *Genesis*: masculine

- Second story of creation in *Genesis*: feminine

- Memory of wisdom of elderly man

Day 2:

- Dorothy Day: naturalness of the creative process

- Confirmation of insight to follow journal method and form

- Need for balancing feminine spirit and masculine mind

- Back to the beginning: original sin as disjunction between masculine mind and feminine spirit

Day 3:

- Uncertainty about how to proceed

- Brainstreaming as central to creative process

- Development of stream-of-consciousness in the novel

- Development of brainstorming as a mode of creative problem-solving

- Brainstreaming joining brainstorming and stream-of-consciousness

- Some examples of various uses of brainstreaming

- Brainstreaming as Godlike: *Wisdom* texts balancing the *Genesis* accounts of creation

So what has been the pattern, if any? It seems to me now that my edited and revised brainstreamings have yielded my reasons for wanting to write a book on creativity and spirituality and something of the history of my past unsuccessful attempts to do so. Through discussion with a friend I realized that the block was that I was attempting to write in a method and form that were inappropriate for both my subject and my feminine personality. Recognizing this unconscious error, I asked for guidance in finding an appropriate method and form. The answer to that prayer was the idea of a journal, a concrete recording of the process of development of the book even as it was emerging. The process of writing such a book might mirror the creative process, and the resulting book might embody its subject.

Then I was led deeper into the recognition that God initiates all creativity by creating us in God's image and likeness and by enabling us to create by giving us the Spirit. God's Spirit works naturally in and through us, almost casually, if we but let it. Historically, this Spirit has been stifled by the dominance of masculine mind and needs to be balanced by feminine spirit.

A principal technique for gaining access to our creative spirit is brainstreaming, a combination of stream-of-consciousness and brainstorming. This fundamental technique for eliciting creativity is a manifestation of Wisdom as it is revealed to us in the Wisdom texts of the Old Testament.

Thus, through a process of intuitive and associative thinking, I have sketched something of the nature and history of the creative process in my own life and that of the human race. There does seem to be a pattern emerging. The pattern is clear to me. But will it be clear to minds other than my own? I do not know. Soon I must share what I have written with at least one willing person to see if any of this makes sense and engages anyone else. No one is present at the moment that I can ask to do this for me. So I must wait.

Fidelity to the Waiting Time

While I wait for someone to appear or until I feel moved to seek out such a person, what do I do? I wait. But while I wait, as Progoff says, I do my work. Perhaps this is a point to develop now, this issue of waiting. It has arisen several times in these reflections thus far.

A flood of memories of experiences of waiting arises:

I am fifteen and a high school sophomore studying plane geometry with great intensity. One evening I am struggling to prove a theorem. I work and work, but the answer does not come. In frustration, I give up and decide to go to bed. As my foot touches the top stair, the insight I need dawns. I run back down the stairs to the kitchen table to complete the elusive proof. I only had to wait about thirty seconds – but I had to wait those thirty seconds.

I am forty-nine and struggling with a decision profoundly important to me. I want to do something that external circumstances prevent my doing. In my extreme frustration, I express my helplessness in prayer. An inner voice beneath my turmoil speaks: "Be faithful to the waiting time. Do not worry. Do not plan."

I try as best I can to obey that voice, and after a period of time I am able to do what I wanted to do, although I do it differently from the way I had originally wanted. I had to wait six months this time.

I thought then that the voice was speaking only to that one experience. But reflection on repeated experiences of frustration taught me that it seems to be a general truth guiding me, when what I think I want to do conflicts with what external circumstances permit me to do.

A third example is writing this book. I have had to wait three years.

I have read of similar experiences in the lives of many creative persons. For example, when Isaac Asimov, that prolific writer of science and science fiction, is blocked in his work, he goes to a movie. When he returns to his work, the block has been removed.

A classic example is Archimedes. The emperor has had a bar of gold made into a crown. He believes that the artisan may have cheated him by using an alloy with the gold in making the crown. But he has no way of determining the truth or falsity of his suspicions. The emperor charges Archimedes with solving this. Archimedes goes to the public baths of Syracuse. Sitting in the water, he notices that his body displaces some of the water. Connection: he could determine whether the crown was pure gold or an alloy by putting the crown and a bar of gold the size of the original one in water and then measuring the amounts of water displaced. In his joy, Archimedes runs naked through the streets of Syracuse shouting, "Eureka!" ("I have it!") He had it because he let go of having to have it and waited for it to be given to him. In the meantime, he took a bath.

The literature of creativity is full of such stories of insight achieved after letting go of the search for insight, and waiting. Many times the insight comes in a dream, as it did to Kekule and Lavoisier and Carl Jung. Often, too, it comes during conversation with someone on an unrelated topic or watching an unrelated television program. Part of the mystery: unrelatedness leads to relatedness! But always we must wait for our inner wisdom to make the connection for us, trusting that we do indeed "know more than we understand," as Alfred Adler said.

This process entails acknowledging and accepting our limitations, letting go of conscious attempts to solve the problem, and doing something else while waiting for the answer to be given to us. In studies of the creative process this is called the incubation period. During this mysterious period we give up our conscious attempts to solve a problem. We recognize and accept our limitations. We may say, "To hell with it. I don't care. I can't do it." But in reality we might just as accurately say, "To heaven with it. God cares. God can do it."

When we have acknowledged our human limitations, the problem drops into the unconscious mind, that mysterious realm where Wisdom, the artificer of all, who is mobile beyond all motion, makes the needed and desired connection for us. When we are ready, willing, and able to receive the insight and deal with its consequences, she allows it to pop into our conscious mind when we least expect it. Or she allows it to dawn on us so gently that one day we simply realize it is there.

If we are to be creative, we must learn to do our work as best we can and then let go of it and simply wait for God to do God's part of the work. As the author of *The Cloud of Unknowing* says, "We grow by delays." So, too, do other artworks. We and they grow like a baby in the womb or like seeds in the ground. There is a long period when the seed lies hidden in the earth, germinating but invisible to the surface eye. Then the seed puts forth shoots that gradually break through the surface. The plant continues to develop, bit by bit, and more and more consciously, with periods of growth spurts alternating with seemingly dormant periods. All this time, Wisdom is doing her work while we are doing our work.

Whether we are working with the artwork of our own life or with some other artwork, this waiting time, sometimes brief and sometimes long, must be patiently endured. Yet it is not a time of passive waiting, of simply sitting idly by waiting for a light bulb to light over one's head. No, it is an active time, a time for resting, playing, exercising, and going about the rest of the ordinary business of our lives. But all the time we are engaged elsewhere, we can trust that our problem underneath is being worked out. And then one day (often when we least expect it), some person, some event, or some circumstance will trigger the connection — if we but let it.

This part of the creative process keeps us humble, rooted in *humus*, the earth out of which we are made and of which we remain a part. It keeps us rooted in the reality of our creatureliness. In this creative waiting we are taught patience, and we grow in compassion for all other creatures, even the smallest, who wait with us for the new creation to be fulfilled.

We can and must work hard to be creative. The quality of our connections will be proportionally related to how hard we work, says Rollo May. We must not waste our time and delay our work by indulging in selfish pursuits and surface satisfactions. We must do the best we can with what we have been given.

But in the end, as in the beginning, it is God's work we do. We must learn to do it in God's way, not ours, and in God's time, not our own. We slowly and painfully learn God's way and timing by accepting manifestations of reality other than our own needs, desires, resources, and limitations, even – and most especially – when these objective manifestations of reality frustrate us to the extreme. It must necessarily be so, else we would be God who is ultimate reality and the creative process itself.

3. Unearthing Clues

Evening, July 5: spent most of the day typing, cleaning up, and proofreading the past three days' brainstreaming. Donkey work. But as I did this menial work I also found myself making notes of points that were stimulated as I read:

- Need as the first stage of the creative process

- Spirituality and creativity as co-extensive

- Profile of a creative person: Godlike and simple

- Living creatively as schooling us to respect the freedom of others as our own

- Dealing with frustration

- New communities as a sign of feminine spirit moving now from creating persons to creating groups, the next step in the evolution of global community

Need As Stimulus to Creativity

Later: after dinner, a recent acquaintance and I had an invigorating walk around St. Joseph's Lake, she looking comfortable in her gray zippered sweat shirt and I – sleeveless and sweaterless – striding vigorously to keep warm. We watched for ducklings hatched Sunday in the ground cover in front of the dorm (hatching going on right beneath my window, even as I am "hatching my own duckling"). A refreshing respite from my work.

Of the six items listed above, three attract me now: need, growth of community, and frustration. Let's see what they "hatch" . . .

More and more I recognize that genuine creativity springs from a need, a need in living our lives creatively, in making, in thinking, in doing, or in experiencing. However unconscious or conscious we may be of the need, it is need that creates the disequilibrium or dissonance motivating us to do something to restore our balance and harmony. A need stimulates us to seek the direction that we are to go in reestablishing our balance. A need generates and sustains the energy required to follow that direction.

The more urgent the need, it seems, the greater the energy generated to satisfy it. Connection: That is why the worldwide peace movement is gaining momentum. We need peace, and we need it badly.

Case in point: my need to write you, *Connecting*. I do want to write you, but I sense that I want to because I need to.

At dinner this evening, I met a sensitive young monk. Before long, he asked the frequent question, "Why are you at Notre Dame?" I mumbled, "Just bumming around." A companion added, with a note of kind affirmation, "You are writing a book." Then I heard myself mutter, "I have to get this off my back. Time to move on." Yes, I see it more clearly now. I need to get this over with. I need to take care of old business so that I will be free to move on. Besides, I want to.

Need is crucial to the creative process:

- Shakespeare: how many of his plays did he write, even as they were being produced, because he needed money? How many millions of persons of all cultures have been moved by his plays?

- Picasso: surely he needed to express his own suffering in *Guernica*. How many millions have been moved by this painting?

- Joshua: he wrote the first poems of his life, he said, because he needed to complete an assignment for my creativity course. He had tried to write an essay on Plato and couldn't. Running out of time, he tried his hand at poetry. And the poems flowed. He was overjoyed and couldn't believe he had it in himself. He read some for the class, and the students were delighted to see him come so alive.

- Eloise: she created a dance to a friend's taped voice reading Langston Hughes's "Dream Variations" for the same reason. Her creation of word, music, and dance moved us.

- The atom bomb: Robert Oppenheimer, a Jew, needed to stop the Nazis' annihilation of the Jews during the Second World War. (Where did that example come from?) A perversion of extraordinary gifts? He suffered and repented, saying the team of some of the world's most creative people working on the bomb should have stopped "the day after Trinity." Our gifts are always subject to per-

version. What force kept that destructive dynamic
going after Hitler's defeat? Violence breeding violence. Holocaust spawning holocaust. How to
break that demonic cycle? We don't need it? Or do
we . . . ?

• St. Francis of Assisi's *Canticle of the Sun* and Paul
  Winter's contemporary musical version, *Missa
  Gaia, Earth Mass*: springing from deep need to
  praise God's creation? The poem and the musical
  creation move us.

Need initiates the creative process, a personal need
that, once fulfilled, often has a communal effect. God takes
the initiative to provide something good for the community by implanting a need in an individual person.

Few descriptions of the psychology of the creative process seem to fully recognize that need is what impels us
to creativity in the first place. Most descriptions, stem-
ming from Wallas, describe four stages in that process:
conscious manipulation, incubation, insight, verification
and refinement. They start with the first of the conscious
stages of the process, when in reality creativity begins in
the unconscious.

Most such descriptions have been produced by men and
by psychologists. Could it be they were insufficiently
aware of the role of the feminine spirit in creativity and
did not think to look beneath the surface?

More needs with long-term global implications:

• Teresa's *Interior Castle*: the need for a balanced
  mysticism to counteract the spread of false mysti-

cism in the late Middle Ages. Interest in this work and others is being revived in our time because of a similar need.

- The U.S. Constitution: the need for a system of government appropriate for a democracy.

- Wilbur and Orville Wright's *Kitty Hawk*: the need for global transportation.

- The computer: the need for global memory capacity, paving the way for greater creativity by storing the material to be connected in the creative process.

- Communications satellites: the need for human dialogue on a global scale.

Need sets the process in motion. "Necessity is the mother of invention." Someone beat me to it. Sounds like something Ben Franklin would have said.

But when want exceeds need, greed results, paving the way for squandering the world's resources, and the destruction and breakdown of the creative process.

What the world needs now:

- conservation of resources, material and human.

- unity ("united we stand, divided we fall").

- greater creativity ("the whole is greater than the sum of its parts").

One hopeful response to these needs: small communities now emerging on a global scale.

Community and the Creative Energy Field

Rosemary Haughton sees the phenomenon of small communities springing up everywhere as the sign of the power and presence of the feminine spirit of Wisdom re-creating society. It makes sense. In the first stage of the evolution of the universe, the Spirit concentrated on forming the biosphere, the physical universe. When the peak of that stage was reached, she formed the human person, the bridge from physical to spiritual. Through the great Scriptures of East and West, those manuals of human survival, she provided instruction in the wisdom needed for our wellbeing and protection: Honor the Lord thy God. Keep holy the Sabbath day. Thou shalt not kill. Thou shalt not steal. To reach a goal, give it up. If you see the Buddha on the road, kill him. Be thou holy as the Lord thy God is holy.

But the age of the individual has not achieved Chardin's "noosphere," the spiritual transformation of physical creation. We are in a new age, an Age of Destruction. The forces of destruction have gained momentum over the centuries. They are now too strong to resist one by one. Therefore, we are entering the Age of the New Creation: the Age of the Communion of Saints.

We need each other. We need to band together, helping, encouraging, and sustaining one another. When one is weak, another is strong. If one can think well, another can feel well. If one is depressed, another can dance. If one is lazy, another is industrious. If one is weary, another is refreshed. If one is hungry, another has food; one naked, another has clothing; one homeless, another has shelter to share.

We are all poor. The poor are all those who do not have what we have. Each of us lacks something – time, money, food, joy. In community what I lack is given me, and what I have I share.

One by one we cluster together in our need. Then our small communities will, in turn, cluster together in larger communities. And thus it is that one world, the new creation, is even now coming into being through clusters of communities which are clusters of individual persons.

James Vargiu's model of the creative process, the energy field, is drawn from modern physics and serves well to help us understand this. The physics is beyond me, but the following example gives the drift.

A grade school child experiments with a magnet and iron filings on a piece of cardboard. The child moves the magnet toward the filings. At first, nothing seems to happen. But as the magnet moves closer, individual filings begin to move slightly as each in turn is magnetized. Then slowly, tentatively, the magnetized filings move toward each other, attracted by the magnetic energy infusing each one. The individual filings gather in twos and threes, then form small clusters, increasing the intensity of the magnetic field. Suddenly, when the magnet is at the center and the energy field at its most powerful, the clusters spring together in a pattern of great simplicity and beauty. And so the Spirit is moving in each of us and in our world, drawing all things to itself in a simple and beautiful pattern – if we but let it.

Many of those who have reflected on the creative process have sensed the magnetic field to be a model of the process. Speaking of inspiration in poetry, Plato noted the same analogy in the dialogue, the *Ion*. Teresa of Avila noted it, too, in the metaphor of amber which, when rubbed, attracts straw.

Jesus knew it, too, in his bones:

> And I, if I be lifted up, will draw all things
> to myself.
>
> *John 12: 32*

Teilhard knew it, in his spirit soaring through time and space: love is the affinity of being for being.

On the level of matter, love is easy, I suspect. Particles simply can't resist their attraction to one another. They naturally move with their attractions. But on the level of spirit, love is not often easy. Out of our ignorance, illusion, weakness, and bad will, we resist our attractions. We refuse to allow ourselves to love and to be loved. We refuse to allow ourselves to move and to be moved, to touch and to be touched, in more ways than one. To love, we must be lifted up on the cross. Lifted up, we too will draw all things to ourselves — to our true selves.

The Blessing of Frustration

The cross takes many forms. In creativity, a principal form is frustration. Often we are at cross purposes with ourselves, doing, like St. Paul, what we would not do, and not doing what we would do. Often we are at cross purposes with each other. I want to dance, but my partner does not want to dance with me. My friend wants to see *Return of the Jedi*, and I want to see *Gandhi*. Or we are at cross purposes with circumstances. I want to sew a dress, but the machine breaks down. I want to redecorate the living room, but can't afford a plasterer. I want to balance the checkbook, but the walk needs shoveling, the washing needs doing, and the dinner needs cooking. When I am crossed, I am cross and crossing.

Dealing with a frustration, major or minor, is a critical moment in the creative process of producing a work of art, whether it is the artwork of our lives or another project. If I give up in my frustration, the work will never come to be. If I take my frustration out on the work, the violence will distort the work. If I take my frustration out on myself or another, my creative energy and the other's is diminished, and the artwork of our lives is diminished.

But if I attend to the causes and results of my frustration, if I listen to all that it is telling me, and accept the reality of my situation and surrender to its demands, things at cross purposes will draw together at the center of the cross, the "still point of the turning world." At that center I and my work will be at peace because I have allowed all reality to be as it is. I have not tried to force reality into acceding to my wishes and needs.

This morning I determined to share my writing to this point with someone. I felt I needed to do so. I was growing fearful, afraid I was far out in left field, in danger of being lost or, at the least, of wasting my time and energy. Uncertainty, insecurity, anxiety – the old familiar, insidious forces of self-destruction – had begun to poke up their heads to taunt me and frighten me out of continuing my work.

I called a friend, hoping to ask her to give me her response to my work. She was not in. I left my number, asking that she return my call. She did not call back. Then frustration, too, began to gnaw at me. But I recognized her for what she is, "an old bitch gone in the teeth."

Common sense rescued me from those toothless jaws. Let the old bitch gum away. Meanwhile, no hurry; I will reach my friend another day. Or ask another friend to evaluate my work. Or trust my own judgment. In the meantime, I can do other things, any number of other things: eat, walk, read, write letters, take a nap, wash the dishes, call a sick friend, listen to music. Thinking of these things calms me, and I continue my work.

When I later read the script, I was glad that I had not been able to reach my friend. After all, the work was progressing, I was enjoying much of it, and I was learning as I wrote. No matter if anyone else likes it or finds it useful. As Eliot said, "For us, there is only the trying,/ the rest is not our business."

Such moments of frustration are golden in the work of making an artwork of our own lives. In living the frustrations, in dealing with them creatively, we sharpen our interior senses, those delicate senses of inner seeing, touching, tasting, hearing, and feeling. We strengthen the muscles of our spirit. Such moments properly attended to bring with them all the fruits of waiting mentioned earlier: humility, patience, compassion, and psychic and spiritual stamina. If we are ever to experience the full joy of "I have it," we must first experience the pain of "I don't have it." Our *Eureka* is all the more joyous for our *Ouch*.

Morning, July 6: dialogue with *Connecting: Creativity and Spirituality* as an artwork.

Brief focusing statement: *Connecting* and I have been having a honeymoon, of sorts, these past few days. We have been pretty much alone together, getting to know each other at a deeper level. I feel that we are compatible and should stick together for awhile longer.

Me: Good morning, *Connecting*. How are you today?

C: I feel fine. How about you, Christian?

Me: I do, too. What would you like to do today?

C: I'd like you to type up what we did together yesterday.

Me: Anything else?

C: Well, let's see. Where do we go from here?

Me: Maybe go back and reread everything from the point where I last summarized you?

C: Sounds good to me. That will give us our bearings. Then we can see the direction to proceed.

Me: Makes sense to the old English teacher in me.

C: Me, too. That's how things usually proceed, isn't it? A cycle of work and rest, recapitulation and refinement. Then rest and moving on into another cycle.

Me: Yes. Evolution is cyclical.

C: Yeats thought that, too. His works are full of im-
     ages of the gyre. Like the "Second Coming":

> Turning and turning in
>   the widening gyre
> The falcon cannot hear
>   the falconer;
> Things fall apart; the centre
>   cannot hold;
> Mere anarchy is loosed upon
>   the world,
>
>   . . .
>
> The best lack all conviction,
>   while the worst
> Are full of passionate intensity.

Me: That was a prophetic poem, presaging the end of
     the cycle of this past two thousand years in his-
     tory.

C: It also contains a clue to keeping the center to-
     gether.

Me: What is that?

C: The best must recover all conviction.

Me: How can they do that?

C: Through single-minded attention to the creative
     process that can reverse the cycle of destruction.

Me: How will that do it?

C: Simone Weil had a key in that essay on education for the love of God. As I remember, she said that paying close attention to any study, no matter the subject, prepares one for prayer. Prayer opens us to the creative.

Me: Makes sense. "Be attentive" is Lonergan's first transcendental imperative, the first level of consciousness. Higher levels of consciousness build on this. That's why "Be here now" is such good advice. *Being – here – now* is remaining *in* the present moment, experiencing it, living it. By being *here*, where we happen to find ourselves, rather than *there*, somewhere we might prefer to be, we are in the flow of process, and it can carry us with it in its forward movement through the cycle. "Bloom where you are planted."

C: Not bad, Christian. I see similar connections. To put it in your language, "Keep on truckin'."

Me: Or as a teacher quoted Faber, "For God's sake, don't sit down." I like that.

C: As Progoff puts it, "The most important experience is the next one." All those folks had a similar insight into the nature of the process of creativity: dynamic, powerful, forward moving, evolutionary.

Me: Funny. That last sentence stops me. I don't know what to say next.

C: Then don't *say* anything. Do something. Time
     now to stop our talking and go to work. You al-
     ready have your instructions from yesterday's
     material; try to see how things tie together. Then
     you will be able to sense the direction of my for-
     ward movement. And after you rest awhile, you
     will have the energy to go forward with me, if you
     get the drift.

Me: Makes sense. Catch you later.

C: Good enough.

Feelings while writing: I felt that the dialogue flowed
easily. Just a little of Miss Grundy in it, wanting to stop
the flow with some editing. But I managed to squelch her.
She will have her way in due time.

New thoughts stirred on reading the dialogue: reading
what I had written on "Be here now," I connected with
Jerzy Kosinski's book/movie, *Being There*. Interesting
connection. Chance, the main character, as I remember,
was never *here* but always *there* – somewhere outside himself – thus in unreality. Dull. Stupefied. He was drawn
into the center of power, the U.S. Presidency. But I do not
remember just how the book ended. Funny. I must check
out that connection sometime. Where do I go next in this
journal? Do as I have been told: type, summarize, get my
bearings for moving on.

Summing Up

Later: summary of a summary, pp. 31 - 32 :

- I need to write this book.

- It had been blocked through my trying to impose an inappropriate method and form on it.

- The appropriate method and form is that of a journal recording the process of the book's coming to be as it comes to be.

- God initiates all creativity.

- Historically, the process of creativity has been distorted by the dominance of the masculine mind.

- A principal technique for gaining access to the creative process is brainstreaming.

Recapitulation of ideas developed from the evening of Day 3 to the morning of Day 5:

Evening of Day 3:

- Learning how to wait is a necessary part of the creative process.

- Waiting allows our inner wisdom to work and increases humility, patience, and compassion.

Day 4:

- A need initiates the creative process.

- A major need today is development of community.

- Love is the magnetic energy drawing all things in the universe together.

- Dealing with frustration is necessary to complete a creative work. It also increases sensitivity, humility and psychic and spiritual stamina.

Day 5:

- Evolution moves through cycles of creativity and destructiveness.

- Attentiveness to the present moment keeps us in the cyclic movement, keeps us rooted in reality.

Analysis

What pattern, if any, can I discern in this distillation of over forty pages of writing?

- Need, frustration, insight into causes of frustration, insight into ways out of frustration.

- God initiates creativity; process distorted by dominance of the masculine mind; brainstreaming a practical way to actualize the feminine mind and restore balance to the process; necessity of waiting.

- Need initiates the creative process; process moves in cycles; attentiveness keeps us in the process.

Thus there seem to have been roughly three cycles operating in the work of these five days:

- In the first cycle, I tell the story of the personal history of this book's needing and wanting to come to be.

- In the second cycle, I begin with the source of creativity as revealed in some of the Scriptures, discuss a major breakdown in the process, and consider brainstreaming and learning to wait as practical ways to restore the balance in the process.

- In the third cycle, I double back to reinterpret need as initiating the cyclic process that moves us with it, if we stay in it through attending to living the present moment.

However accurate or inaccurate this analysis of the emerging pattern may be, it does give me a sense of where I have been and of how I and this book have come to be where we are. Now where do we go from here?

I sense a need to clarify *want* and *need* as they relate to creativity. That is the only question that engages me at the moment. But I am too tired to address it now. I need to take a break – maybe a long one – before I attempt it.

Satisfaction vs Value

Morning, July 7: this morning's waking brought no new ideas on *what* to write, but it did bring an idea on *how* to write. Perhaps it is time now that I disciplined myself to write directly on the word processor. This bears some reflecting upon, because I am most comfortable writing in a relaxed position with a felt-tip pen and my paper fastened to a clip board. I like it this way.

But writing directly on the word processor would conserve time and energy. Word processing what I have already written by hand obviously takes additional time – the time of writing and the time of word processing. It also takes more energy: my own because of the duplication of my efforts, the energy of the trees and manufacturing that go into the making of paper, and the electrical energy consumed by the word processor.

So the method of writing I most enjoy consumes considerable energy. Adopting a new method of writing should consume less energy. I am faced here with a question of satisfaction and a question of value.

Since the time I have left for writing this book seems limited to the next two weeks, I need to consider this. Secondly, being creative means being open to the new, even new ways of working. But this, in turn, means changing habits developed over a long period of time – not easy, by any means.

The prospect cannot be dismissed out of hand. It needs considering. Perhaps a reasonable compromise: do both . . . as I feel so moved. Write as I most enjoy writing and also write in a way that is most conserving of time and energy. In time, perhaps I will find that writing directly on the word processor will become more natural to me and prove to be as enjoyable as composing with a pen in hand. We will see.

Need vs Want

The point that presented itself yesterday remains with me: explore the relationship between *need* and *want* in the creative process. It seems to be clearly established that need initiates the creative process. We create something or allow it to be created in us because we need it. The need may be unconscious or conscious, but it is need that generates and sustains the energy to create.

Our needs, then, are a manifestation of God's initiative in the world. The more aware we are of our own and others' needs, the more we experience God in our life.

If I create only what I need to create, I am using only those resources that are necessary. This seems a responsible use of resources. But what if I create what I want but do not need? If I want to create what I need to create, obviously there is no problem. But if I create what I do not need to create, then I am using resources I do not need. Is this responsible?

It would seem not. The time and energy consumed would be taken away from serving my own needs and those of others. Greed? It would seem so. Connection: the movement toward simplicity of life is another manifestation of Wisdom's saving presence in the world.

Wanting to create only what I need to create would seem to be a most responsible exercise of freedom. Wanting to create what is not necessary would seem to be an irresponsible exercise of freedom. Yet we are made to do what we want. That is our freedom – and our responsibility. But often we do not know what we really want, let alone what we really need. This is not an easy matter to decide.

Did God create the world because God wanted to do it, or did God need to do it? Surely God does not need to do anything. Yet by its nature love wants to share its being with others. God needs to share God's being with the world. So in God need and want are one?

If so, it should be the same with us who are made in the image and likeness of God. We should want to do what we need to do and only that. Yet we are free to do as we like.

This question seems beyond me. I do not have a clear notion. Creating what I or another needs seems the most responsible response of freedom. Creating what I or another want but does not need may be irresponsible. I must wait and see. In the meantime, I want and need to get on with this book.

Yesterday's work brought a completion of three cycles of thought and started me on a fourth with this discussion of the relationship between need and want in creativity. Now where do I go from here?

I am blocked. I do not know how to proceed. I sense that I need to straighten up my room; entropy has taken over and scattered papers everywhere. I also need to take care of some other matters. So I will do these necessary things while I wait.

Openness: The Fertile Ground of Creativity

Wimpleton and Noelle: A Story

Lovely is the June afternoon and pleasant is the company. My sister, Jean; her sister-in-law Thelma; two of my grandnieces, Noelle and Tracy, and I are driving from Maryland to Pennsylvania. The two little girls, five and three, are going to spend a few days with their grandparents while their mother tends to newly born Jullie Ann and baby brother Joshua.

As I drive, Jean sits in the back, trying to entertain and contain her grandchildren. In an effort to help, I introduce Wimpleton, visiting from Wimbledon, England. Wimpleton is not a wimp, but an engaging fellow. Just now he sits on the roof of the car, his feet dangling over the windshield in front of my eyes. Soon he crawls over to the right window. As I describe his antics, Tracey, a bright-eyed, earth-solid child, strains to see him. She is utterly perplexed. Noelle "sees" him immediately and enters into the story, freely adding to Wimpleton's repertoire of tricks.

Soon Noelle introduces four friends: Cammy, Melanie, Anna, and Russell. Throughout the rest of the journey, these five imaginary friends join us now and then to entertain us. Noelle explains that Wimpleton is a "fake man," and eventually Tracy catches on to the little fantasy.

The following morning I prepare to leave my sister's home to return to Detroit. I have enjoyed getting to know the two grandnieces that I seldom have an opportunity to see. Saying good-bye, I tell them that I will miss them as I drive on alone. Immediately, a new light modulates Noelle's soft brown eyes.

"You won't be alone," she says.

"I won't?" I respond.

"No." Noelle continues. "*Your* friend and *my* friends will be with you."

At that, I name them, one by one. "Cammy and Melanie

and Anna and Russell – and who is the fifth?"

Sweetness turns up the corners of Noelle's lips as she prompts me: "Wim-ple-ton!"

I was touched that a child of five could make such a connection. Instantaneously sensing my need and making an appropriate response, she offers me what I need and what she has to give: the companionship of our imaginary characters on my continuing journey.

I recall this story now because it illustrates how a creative response to a need – the need to entertain children during a long trip – can blossom in a charity that returns to shelter us in its branches. I sense a new creation. My relationship with Noelle is different and deeper, I suspect.

When we are open to the present moment and respond to it, surprising things can happen because openness is a key to creativity. It makes sense that it is so. If God always initiates the creative process, we must be open to receiving the initiative. If we want to accept an initiative, we can do so by being alert to the need of the moment and responding to it as best we can. God manifests initiative through our wants and needs.

Yet how closed we so often are to our own needs as well as to those of others. Preoccupied with our selfish desires, we are like an acorn – a hard shell encasing the real need – which is the seed of new life, if we but knew it. The seed will decay unless we allow it to break through the shell. Regretting a past action or anticipating a future one, we so easily miss the present open moment that contains hidden within it the needs which are the seeds of future possibilities.

As the poet Jessica Powers wrote, whoever lives outside the Eternal Now "slides down wastes of time." So much of our living is not really living, and much is escape from living. As Eliot says, we go about our lives "living and partly living." Sooner or later, the unlived moment comes back to haunt us, all too often crippling us with guilt.

Guilt vs Sorrow

Brooding on such guilt is a destructive response that only breeds more unlived moments. Guilt mires us in the past and poisons the present. Sorrow sweetens the present and seeds the future with new opportunity to do other than what we did to acquire guilt. As a friend once kindly said in response to an apology, "I'll know how sorry you are the next time."

A creative response to guilt is to acknowledge the waste, accept it as part of the darkness that shadows each of us, and redeem our guilt by living the present moment more fully. This is creative sorrow.

Sorrow

The broken window,
The cracked vase,
The trampled rose:
Let them be as they are,
The past be as it is.
Guilt scatters salt
Among yesterday's ashes
While sorrow's tears
Sprout willows
Between the shards.

4. Consulting an Authority

Morning, July 8: I slept well last night. The long walks, the picnic with a friend by St. Mary's Lake, and the gathering of Mercy sisters last evening were refeshing. Before sleeping I reread Flannery O'Connor's introduction to *A Memoir of Mary Ann*. A stunning piece of prose, so straight and true and direct. Upon waking, I decided my first work of the day should be to reread all that I have written so far. I have been getting my act together fairly well. Now seems a good time to clean it up, see if I can purify my prose style through the filter of Flannery's.

Later: dialogue with Flannery O'Connor as a Wisdom Figure:

Me: Well, Flannery, walking back from lunch just now, a woman asked me to recommend a journal exercise. I suggested that she dialogue with a wisdom figure in her life, asking that person, "Have you anything to say to me?" Connection: it is time for *me* to consult with a wisdom figure myself. It was a toss-up between you and Teresa. You won, Flannery.

F.: Well, Christian, that insight makes me nauseous – but what can I do for you?

Me: You can tell me what you think of this book I am writing. You know that I respect and value your opinion.

F.: Yes, I know, and I appreciate that. I guess I would want to say just be as simple and direct and straight as you can, in your thoughts, your action, and your prose.

Me: You certainly seemed to be those things. Those are the qualities that most appeal to me in your work, especially in your letters and your introduction to *A Memoir for Mary Ann*.

F.: I liked that, too. It surprised me, too, how that event turned out.

Me: Surprise is a good sign, isn't it, in creativity?

F.: Certainly. When we are surprised by something that comes to us, we can be reasonably sure that it comes from a depth beneath the conscious mind. That is why it surprises us. We were not conscious of it. When it comes to the surface and we accept it, it is conscious. Then we can integrate it, if we want to. When something remains unconscious to us, it remains unintegrated. When something is integrated, it drops back into the unconscious, and we can genuinely forget about it and move on.

Me: And in an artwork other than our lives, Flannery? How does that work?

F.: In a similar way. As I said in a letter, "I write what I am given." It is not usually given whole, however. It comes to me bit by bit when I open myself to my unconscious depths. I am free, of course, to do whatever I like with what is offered to me.

Me: Sometimes you work with it, and sometimes you don't.

F.: Right. I usually just go with it as I sense it wants to go. As I go with it, I pay attention to myself as well as to the work. If I find that I can work with it freely and peacefully, I can be pretty sure that it is a work I am to follow further. If not, then I am probably not meant to do the work, at least at this time. It was probably a figment of my imagination, a fantasy, not real work.

Me: But easily doesn't mean no struggle or pain.

F.: Not at all. There may very well be much of both, but there are also the motivation and energy and direction that make it possible for me to move forward with the work. The combination of ease and struggle blend into peace with myself and peace with the work.

Me: That makes sense – the creative tension.

F.: Yes. One without the other is no good. If there is only ease, the work is likely to be superficial. If there is only struggle, the work is probably too hard for me. It is beyond my gifts and competence.

Me: That makes sense, too, It reminds me of the Dalai Lama in that *Rolling Stone* interview I read. He said that he was so happy when he was discovered, as a small child, to be the fourteenth reincarnation of the Dalai Lama. At first, I was surprised – so much responsibility for one so young. Not to mention anyone's dreaming of being divine! Yet he must have felt within himself the capacity to fulfill the demands of that office; therefore, he was happy because both capacity and opportunity came together for him.

F.: It is true for each of us, if less dramatically so. We aren't all Dalai Lamas. We have to be ourselves and do our own work. That's it in a nutshell, Christian. Don't try to be somebody else, and don't try to do somebody else's work. That is for them to do, not you. And they can't be you or do your work. It is as simple as that.

Me: It is simple. I keep being drawn back to simplicity in creativity. That seems a hallmark of genuine creativity.

F.: It is, in both the process and the work that results. Keep things simple because they are meant to be simple, coming from God and reflecting God as they do.

Me: That doesn't mean simplistic.

F.: Not at all. The simplistic is superficial. The simple comes from the depths. The simple can contain within itself the most complex elements. But that is it. It *contains* those elements. They are integrally joined in the most simple possible whole. There is nothing extra, nothing not needed, and there is nothing missing, nothing needed for the whole. It just is, and it is just right. And you know that it is right. You sense it. When you feel something awry, pay attention to that. It is trying to tell you that a piece is missing, or extra – or out of place.

Me: That is a heap of words for you, Flannery.

F.: That's because you are not where I am. You are not simple enough for me to communicate with you in a few words.

Me: Or in no words?

F.: Right. When we really get simple, there are no words because we don't need any. We can communicate just as well without them, so why bother?

Me: But in the meantime we need words.

F.: We do, and so we use them as best we can. Words were my way of communicating with the world.

Me: And helping it come to be a better world.

F.:   I hope so.

Me: Many people certainly appreciate your stories
     and letters. You have entertained us and taught
     us much about creativity and spirituality.

F.:   If so, I am grateful. I was just doing what I had
     to do. And I was grateful for those who helped
     me do it.

Me: So must each of us do what we have to do and
     with gratitude for those who help us.

F.:   That makes for a happier world, it seems to me.
     It cuts out all that manipulating and using
     people for one's own ends. We each have our
     own life's project to complete before we die, but
     we are not meant to complete it alone. We are
     meant to seek help when we need it, and people
     are willing and able to give it. And we in our
     turn do the same for others. Be sure people are
     willing; otherwise, you are using them. And be
     sure they are free; otherwise, you manipulate
     them.

Me: An artwork is never really the work of one per-
     son.

F.:   Right. It is just that one person usually sees the
     thing through. But there are also corporate
     artworks that spring from a corporate need.
     Like everything else in creation, artworks are
     becoming more complex.

Me: We do what we are given to do; and if we are smart, we do it simply, and we simply do it.

F.:   Don't think too much about it, Christian. Just do it. If it was the right thing, you will eventually know that. If it was the wrong thing, you will eventually know that, too. So why worry? Just live.

Me: Makes sense. Just live.

F.:   That is what it's all about, you know. You only have one life, so live it as best you can.

Me: I'm trying.

F.:   I think you are. You're not doing too badly. This book is part of your living and part of your work. So be on with both, in peace.

Me: Thanks, Flannery. I needed that.

F.:   Not really. You knew it yourself before I even said it to you. You wouldn't have been able to hear it otherwise. It is just that in this instance I am the means that God chose to make you conscious of what is already in you.

Me: Aren't we marvels, each of us?

F.:   Some of us are monsters, you know. Or haven't you read my stories?

Me: Sure I have. I guess I would say that each of us has a monster or two within us. That is why it's so important that we express ourselves. Then the monsters can make themselves known to us, and we can tend to them. A monster properly attended to becomes "an old bitch gone in the teeth," no harm to anyone.

F.: In my stories I tried to dramatize that none of us is a saint. In this life, we are all sinners, imperfect and distorted, sometimes grotesque. The saints were no better than the rest of us, just different, in that they recognized and accepted the monsters within them and went about living their lives as best they could. No more, no less. It was as simple as that. And it still is.

Me: No big deal, Flannery.

F.: No big deal, Christian.

Cleaning Up and Clearing Out

Morning, July 9: yesterday I spent most of my working time refining my style and typing. It was a good chance to practice what I have been preaching about dealing with frustration. Ran into problems because I tried to put too much material on one disk. I had to go back and redo a considerable portion.

But I remained peaceful throughout, took strategic breaks to walk, eat, pray, talk, and watch the news and a *Mash* rerun. I awoke this morning again feeling refreshed, so all signs seem go for another day of work.

Waking brought some new ideas to be developed, but I sense that it would be good to continue my clean-up operation today. It will feel good to have a sense of this part tentatively completed. I may find that I want to do a little more refining later, but the nature of this book is such that I do not want to make any major structural changes. The basic process is what it is, and I will let it be. I sense the book is about half written, at least. It will be interesting to see if that turns out to be the case.

Courage

Later: courage. I haven't said anything about courage, and creativity takes much courage. From the Latin *cor*: "heart," and the Middle English *corage*: "the heart as the seat of feeling." To create we have to take heart, have heart, and be heart. "We gotta have heart." Courage is at the heart of the matter. Courage is at the heart of matter, struggling and surging toward fulfillment and beyond.

In his lovely book, *The Courage to Create*, Rollo May explores the need for courage. He makes sense. Every creative act is also an act of destruction. Every new thing that comes into existence rises out of the ashes of something old. The seed is destroyed as the plant grows out of it. The egg shell is broken as the duckling staggers blinking into the light. The new start in a relationship grows out of shattered dreams and broken promises.

Courage to start . . . The creative act is a step into the void. We don't really know where the impetus originates. It rises up from our depths, sometimes frightening us with what it will require of us in commitment and energy. A work begun takes on a life of its own and makes demands of us.

Courage to continue . . . We don't know where we will get the resources to go forward. We don't know how we will find our way. We sometimes get lost and find ourselves in a blind alley, or up a tree, or in a ditch. Sometimes, too, we find ourselves in the light, and that can be frightening. The work underway remains a constant companion, nagging at us for attention.

Courage to complete the work . . .   We don't know where it will all end, but we suspect that wherever it ends, that ending is just another beginning, paving the way for yet another step into another void. And the work completed has its own destiny. Our works, like children, are "hostages to fortune." "Go, litel bok," said Chaucer. "Go, little book," said Merton to *Raids on the Unspeakable*. Once the work is completed, it goes out into the world to do its own work, and we no longer have any control over it. Yet a part of us goes with it.

No wonder we hesitate to begin. No wonder we falter along the way. No wonder we take a deep breath at the end. Well we might. As someone said to me, "You'd better think twice." It takes a great deal of courage to feel our way in the dark.

But we are made in the image and likeness of God. How much courage did it take for God to create the world in the first place? How much courage did it take to continue creating it after we humans appeared on the scene with a freedom like God's to do as we wish? How much courage does it take for God to remain faithful to the commitment to remain with us to see our co-creation through to the end?

Such courage is rooted in faith – the faith Julian of Norwich possessed: "All shall be well, and you will see for yourself that all manner of things shall be well." Faith fuels courage.

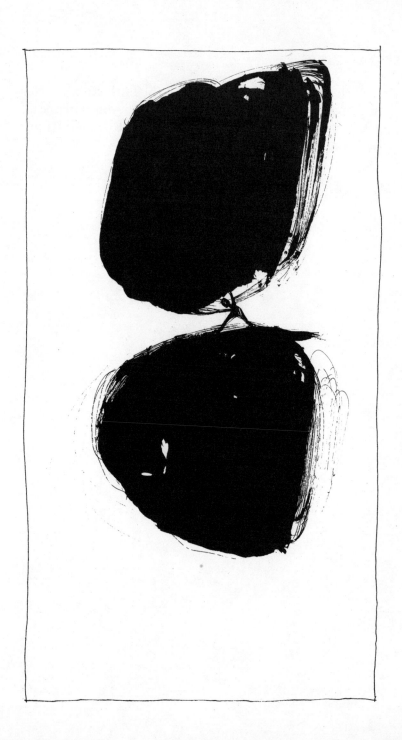

5. Neurotic Fear vs Holy Fear

July 11 - 13: It has been two days since I composed any new material. I have spent most of my working time typing and cleaning up a good copy of the first fifty-five pages to send to a good friend. I called her on Sunday to see how her dad was doing after surgery. We talked of many things, including *Connecting*. She caught on right away to what I am trying to do and affirmed me in it. Her enthusiasm was such that I asked her if she would read some of it and give me her response. She was obviously happy to do that, and I would like that. We are close friends, so I really trust that she will be truly objective. She would not want me to make an ass out of myself.

I also took a good bit of time off yesterday and today to rest and walk and visit. Sticking to Ozzie D., my word processor, for long periods of time is tiring and hard on the shoulder muscles.

While walking just now, I found myself reflecting on fear, the stimulus to courage. We face two kinds of fear in creating, neurotic fear and holy fear. It is important that we learn to distinguish between them.

Neurotic fear stems from the surface of the psyche. Like guilt, it is destructive. This is the fear that prevents us from being all that we can be and doing all that we can do. It haunts us, plagues us with worry over "what if" and "maybe." It draws us into abusing our imagination by playing with figments, fears that have no real teeth in them. Neurotic fear stirs up butterflies in our stomachs.

If neurotic fear is severe, we may need to seek professional counseling. If the fear makes us mildly uncomfortable, chances are that the best way to fight it is to act in spite of it. We can be pretty sure that we should do the thing that neurotic fear is telling us not to do. Because that is its purpose: to destroy us and our work. If we want to destroy ourselves and our work, we have only to obey our neurotic fears.

But if we conquer a neurotic fear, we find that it, too, becomes "an old bitch gone in the teeth." As we get to know it for what it is, we can go about our business while the old bitch gums away. She can't hurt us – unless we let her. Those toothless jaws have no power to bite and devour us.

But holy fear is another matter. We should be alert to holy fear, too, because it comes from a deeper level within us than the psyche. Holy fear comes from our spirit. Holy fear strikes at us bone deep. It comes from our spirit of wisdom. Our spirit knows better than we do what is good for us and what is bad. Our spirit can smell real danger, and it alerts us to danger by arousing a holy fear.

A constant theme of the New Testament is, "Have no fear." The fear Jesus was referring to is neurotic fear. Jesus was saying, "Do what you have to do, no matter how afraid you feel."

Retracing the Ground to Find Direction

Evening, July 12: I sense that it is time for another summary. Time to go back and retrace the ground covered since the last summary and pick up direction from there.

July 7:

- I should consider trying to acquire the habit of composing directly on Ozzie D.

- Need initiates the creative process.

- I do not have a clear notion of the distinction between need and want in the creative process.

- The story of Wimpleton and Noelle illustrates how responding to a need often brings blessings back to us.
- Really living is living in the present moment.

- Guilt is destructive; sorrow is creative.

July 8:

- I need to take time to purify the style of the writing done to this point.

July 9:

- Simplicity and surprise are hallmarks of the creative process.

- Creative works are given to us bit by bit.

- Ease and struggle are in creative tension.

- Creativity requires helping relationships.

- All of us have monsters within us.

- Creativity requires courage.

July 11:

- Neurotic fear is destructive; holy fear is creative.

As I analyze the above summary, I do not see any particular pattern emerging. I do notice several distinctions:

- need/want.

- sorrow/guilt.

- the simple/the simplistic.

- holy fear/neurotic fear.

Making Distinctions

Considering these distinctions, I am most attracted by the timing. This book began with recognizing the critical distinctions that helped break through the blocks preventing me from writing. While writing, I have made other distinctions. But making distinctions seems to pervade this latest stage.

This strikes me as a natural development. As Whitehead said, "Style is the last acquirement of the educated mind." Concern for the cultivation of style properly comes late in the process of creativity.

Learning to bat a ball, a baseball player first concentrates on learning to control the swing: the important thing is to connect bat and ball. After she acquires a measure of control over her swing, she concentrates on developing power so that she can hit the ball farther. When she has acquired some measure of control and power, she concentrates on developing her style – learning to swing not only accurately and powerfully but also with ease and grace.

Control, power, style .... All three are present to some degree at every stage, but we give concentrated attention to developing them one by one.

Cultivating style is a matter of precision. Whatever the art form, making distinctions helps us become more precise. In living creatively, we become more precise in distinguishing the relevant from the irrelevant, the significant from the insignificant data involved in our choices. In morality, we become more precise in responsible action. In philosophy and science, we become more precise in seeing the distinctions among truths. In the arts, we become more precise in making distinctions among pigments, forms, tones, movements, and words.

Precision is a matter of being aware of subtleties. We begin to see subtle differences where once we saw only an indistinct blur. The more precise we are and the more distinctions we see, the more subtle we become in both creating and appreciating.

The amateur painter is aware of only a few shades and tints of blue, seeing only light blue, medium blue, dark blue. The accomplished painter recognizes the distinctions between shades and tints of cerulean blue, Prussian blue, cobalt blue, baby blue, sky blue, and a host of others. The accomplished dancer, sculptor, musician, poet, or thinker perceives subtle discordancies and harmonies that do not register with a person less accomplished in the art form.

Thus our exterior senses of sight, taste, touch, hearing, and smell become keener. Our interior senses, too, become more alert. We become more aware – the first level of consciousness. We have life more abundantly. We live more humanly.

With this increasing capacity for subtle distinctions, we begin to acquire a discerning heart, a heart that can better distinguish shades of difference between reality and illusion, truth and falsity, good and evil, love and disunity. We begin to be able to make our way through the confusion of values that distinguishes our time in history.

As we become more and more aware of subtle distinctions, we also become more aware of fundamental likenesses. We see how things are alike and different, and we appreciate their likenesses and differences more. We realize the value of diversity within unity. We value young and old, rich and poor, black and white, male and female. We see that all things are one in being, one not in uniformity but in unity, a unity that contains differences in harmony. More and more we see and value the richness of texture in all of life.

Living in Hope

This openness to distinctions also helps us have hope in the midst of despair. Hope enables us to transcend the bad news because we believe that the good news will ultimately prevail. Hope helps us to transcend the evidence of appearances and see the evidence of reality. Hope enables us to trust that appearances shall not be decisive.

Such hope is a gift. But like other gifts, it is seldom given in one lump sum. More often, it is given bit by bit through concrete experiences of hope. The more alert we are to distinctions, the more alert we will be to signs of hope and the better we will be able to cultivate the signs of hope and resist the signs of despair. Hope is creative; despair is destructive. One of the greatest needs of our time is hope.

Writing is a process of seeing relationships and making discoveries. As I have been writing this past week, I have become more and more aware of signs of hope in our time. Each of them, however, coexists with a sign of despair. None of them, like none of us, is pure. It is easy to despair if we see indistinctly. If we are to sustain ourselves in hope, we must cultivate our ability to see and make distinctions.

Twelve signs of hope in the midst of despair:

- Much of the feminist movement is harsh and abrasive, but it is also bringing to consciousness our critical need to resist male domination and reclaim the feminine spirit.

- Some communities, like Jonestown, are destructive cults; yet small communities are an important step in the emergence of a global community.

- Computers can be isolating and dehumanizing,

yet they also increase the memory capacity available for unprecedented creativity.

- Supersonic jets move with unnatural noise and speed, yet they also make possible global transportation.

- Communications satellites pollute the atmosphere and endanger the earth, but they also make possible global communications.

- Modern science can distort and destroy matter, but it is also discovering the reality of spirit.

- Modern psychology can be used for manipulation and brainwashing, but it also helps free us from neurosis and psychosis.

- Massive unemployment is tragic, but it can also bring us to reconsider our values and simplify our lives.

- Modern economics continues to oppress and exploit the poor, but it also can devise systems for a more just and equitable distribution of goods.

- Altering states of consciousness to escape from reality through abuse of drugs is destructive, but this abuse is telling us that human beings need the expanded and deepened consciousness that opens us to reality. Such altered states of consciousness can safely be attained through contemplative prayer and a disciplined life style.

- Journal writing can take us around in a vicious circle, but it can also help us break through the circles of self-destructiveness.

- Theological reflection on experience calls much of established tradition into question, but it can also bring us closer to the truth.

If the signs of hope are to prevail over the signs of despair, we good people everywhere must get "off our duffs" and on to our destinies. We must sacrifice jobs and careers to vocations. We must sacrifice the pursuit of money to the pursuit of quality of life. We must sacrifice power over others to service of others. We must sacrifice dog-eat-dog competition to human-help-human cooperation. We must sacrifice the satisfaction of superficial desires to the fulfillment of our hearts' deepest desires.

In short, we must discover our real needs and our real gifts. Our real needs can initiate the creative process. Our gifts indicate to us the particular realms of creativity that are most authentic for us. Using real gifts to serve real needs is authentic creativity, a creativity capable of reversing the cycle of destruction currently prevailing on a global scale.

We must each of us commit ourselves single-mindedly to the creative use of whatever gifts we have been given, in the service of whatever needs present themselves to us. The gifts are in us because we are made in the image and likeness of God. The gifts of creativity in science, technology, economics, psychology, communications, politics, and spirituality that we so desperately need today are even now within particular human beings. Each of us must claim our gifts, develop them, and use them for the world's sake, for God's sake, and not least of all for our own sake. By claiming and using our gifts in the service of others, we save our own souls.

Single-Mindedness and Emergent Creativity

In his book *The Practice of Process Meditation*, Ira Progoff distinguishes between *core creativity* and *emergent creativity*. Core creativity is ordinary creativity, the kind of creativity that I have been talking about for the most part in this book. It is the process of connecting that brings something new into being. It is a natural, nonrational – but rationally controlled – process that we can enter into to bring about the creation of a particular artwork.

Emergent creativity is outside our direct control. In emergent creativity "something extra" happens, something that was not anticipated and cannot be deliberately made to happen. As examples of emergent creativity, Progoff cites the Buddha's "Diamond Sutra" and St. Francis of Assisi's "Canticle of the Sun."

As I understand him, Progoff discerns that the distinguishing characteristic of emergent creativity is single-minded dedication to making an artwork of one's life. Such single-minded devotion radically opens persons to receiving creative works that are beyond their ordinary capacities. They cannot will such works into being or bring them about solely through their own efforts. They simply happen. And they happen when and where they happen. But single-mindedness in authentic living seems to create an environment where "something extra" *can* happen.

I believe that this concept of emergent creativity may be significant for our times on a communal and even global scale. If one person can be radically open to emergent creativity's happening, so can a whole group of persons. If a large enough group of persons dedicates itself single-mindedly to authentic community, then "something extra" of communal and even global proportions may happen.

As all of us together single-mindedly go about our real work in whatever ways and in whatever places are possible, we will be a community of persons radically open to emergent creativity. When it will happen and how it will happen, we do not know. We do not know what form it will take. We cannot control it. We cannot make it happen directly. We can only open ourselves radically to receiving it by single-mindedly doing the best we can now with what we have been given – no more, no less. The "something extra" may well be a world peace beyond our imagining.

Despair, Discernment, and Discipline

Later: over lunch, Paddy brought up the "despair of possibilities," and during my long walk after lunch I pondered that. My pondering led, in turn, to considering again the need for discernment of spirits in creativity, the need for discipline, and the modern phenomenon of alienation as a thirteenth sign of hope in the midst of despair.

The despair of possibilities is a distinctly modern phenomenon, another manifestation of the world's evolution toward complexity-consciousness. In earlier periods of history, persons had fewer options and fewer resources.

As a professor of literary theory once noted, Dante was limited in his choices. His limitations enabled him to create the *Divine Comedy*.

Faced with so many options today, we find ourselves unable to choose. If we choose one road rather than another, we suffer the loss of those we did not choose. As a result, we are often paralyzed and choose none.

This is another reason why the precise discernment of spirits becomes more and more necessary in our time. To decide between good and bad is not too difficult. The lines are generally clear. But to choose between the lesser of two evils, or between the good and the better, or the better and the best is another matter. Such choices require the ability to make subtle distinctions, the ability to discern subtle shades of feeling and thought.

Such subtle discernment of spirits, in turn, requires discipline. We need the discipline to attend simultaneously to both external and internal reality. We must discipline ourselves to remain open and alert to all the data available to us, withholding judgment and decision until all the relevant facts are in. Once we know and understand the facts, we need the discipline to resist false dichotomies and allow a pattern of distinctions to form that usually reveals a third way between the extremes. Once we see this pattern, we need the discipline to make a decision based upon our judgment. Once we have decided, we need the discipline to act on our decision, while still remaining open to new data that may alter our decision, however slightly or radically. None of this is easy.

Modern alienation, as I have said, is a mixed blessing. It causes great pain and confusion. But if we allow ourselves to feel our alienation, we generate the energy to resolve the feelings of alienation. We need the discipline to remain in these discordant feelings and allow the natural process of creativity to carry us through them into the cycle of resolution.

As Progoff points out, this can be dangerous. We may be overwhelmed with despair. But it can also be dangerous not to feel our alienation. As we deal with this danger, we must be careful not to falsify the process and not to force it. Falsifying the process or forcing it can have deeply serious consequences.

To seek only the peaks and plateaus and not to experience the valleys is to falsify the process. The peaks and plateaus are defined by the valleys. Our responsible exercise of freedom lies in accepting the nature of the creative process, and in choosing to let it carry us into the valleys of despair as well as to the peaks of joy and the plateau of contentment.

Doing so, we must be very gentle with ourselves and others. We must not force anything, but allow it to move forward in its own way and in its own time. Remaining true to the process and being gentle with it require great discipline and careful discernment of spirits.

While I have been working with this book with such concentration this past week and a half, I have been noticing my own rhythm of work and rest, concentration and relaxation, attention and distraction. Gradually the swings in the cycle have become more gentle. I work for shorter periods of time and take breaks more often. This makes me aware of the importance of self-knowledge in the creative process. The mystics come back again and again to self-knowledge as central to the process of making an artwork of one's life.

And here is a fourteenth sign of hope in our times. Modern developmental psychology is learning a great deal about the stages of the life cycle, the differences between male and female, and the personality differences within the distinctions of sex and stage of life. These three areas of study offer us a great deal in understanding and working with our own creativity.

Developmental studies, such as Erikson's and Kohlberg's, have drawn insights largely from the experiences of men. Some of this is helpful for women and some of it can be harmful. Some of it is helpful, also, to sensitive men – men with strong feminine qualities. But some of it can be harmful to such men.

A number of feminine psychologists, such as Carol Gilligan of Harvard, are now doing similar studies with the experience of women. Gilligan has discovered, for instance, that while most men seem motivated by an ethic of responsibility, most women are motivated by an ethic of caring. While men, and women with strong masculine qualities, seek achievement, for example, women and men with strong feminine qualities are willing to sacrifice achievement for the sake of relationships.

Such knowledge of the stages of human development and individual sexual and personality differences within those stages can help us to discern our own spirits and acquire the discipline proper to us at different stages of our lives. For example, in earlier stages of life a principal task is to develop a strong ego. Later in life, a principal task is to transcend the ego and allow the true self to emerge. As a spiritual director put it, if we do not risk building an idol, the Lord will not find the materials to build an altar. On the other hand, if we grow up too fast, we may find it necessary at a later stage of life to go back to an earlier stage and live out some unfinished business before we can really move forward.

Knowing and accepting ourselves as we are, with our unique sexuality and personality differences at various stages of our lives, we can better discern our spirits, acquire the discipline proper to us, and make the necessary choices. For example, if I am young and energetic, I must be careful not to overextend my energies. If I am young and lazy, I must discipline myself to do my work. If I am older and still ambitious for achievement, I must discipline myself to let go of doing and simply be.

Knowing Oneself and Being Oneself

I once heard a tape of a sister telling her story to a group of sisters in her congregation. She spoke frankly of not having her gifts for leadership affirmed in the congregation, and so she took those gifts elsewhere. She said, "You don't know me. And I don't know you."

I felt that this was perhaps the most profound thing the sister said. It has implications far beyond her own situation. We do not know one another. We do not know one another, because we do not know ourselves. The better I know myself the more sensitive I am to how others are like me and how they are different. The more I know my own needs and gifts, the more I can recognize others' needs and gifts. The more I fulfill my own needs and gifts, the more I am able to encourage others in their creativity. Being fulfilled, I am less likely to be jealous or envious or resentful of another's gifts and less likely to look to them to accomplish what I should accomplish.

Another paradox in the creative process . . . .   The more I know and accept myself, with my gifts and needs and limitations, the more I am one with others. The harder I work at making an artwork of my own life, the more I find myself encouraging and enabling others to make an artwork of their lives.

As I indicated earlier, the twentieth century has been enriched with the growing discovery of the nature and importance of symbols in human growth and transformation. At the same time, we are discovering that there are probably few universal symbols. The crucifix, for example, which is a powerful symbol for Christians, may be meaningless to a Buddhist. The American flag may inspire patriotism in many Americans, but inspire anger and hatred in persons of other nations.

Many persons are coming to believe that the one universal symbol is that of the truly human person. A genuine human being is recognized and accepted anywhere in the world. Seen in this light, making an artwork of one's own life is a consummate act of love for all humankind.

Toward the end of his life, Thomas Merton traveled to Asia to experience for himself the wisdom of the East. Wherever Merton went, he met persons with whom he felt at home. He discovered that beneath the differences of culture and religious doctrine, person can meet and understand and accept person at the level of spirit.

Spirit transcends all differences. Differences are important because each of us becomes who we are within the context of our time and culture. These differences provide the richness of humanity. But beneath all differences, we discover that all human beings are one. We discover more and more the reality that each of us is indeed made in the image and likeness of God. While God expresses God's being differently in an American woman and a Tibetan man, it is one God within both, seeking a diversity of forms of divine self-expression. As we discover the Godlike in ourselves, we also discover the Godlike in others. How can we then fail to serve one another's needs? How can we fail to share one another's gifts?

Connection Between Creativity and Spirituality

Later: as I refined the last few pages, I understood better the truth that broke through the block to this book's coming to be. I can no longer write about creativity in a systematic, analytical, and logical way. Or more precisely, for me the systematic, analytical, and logical must be subsumed in the organic. Allowing the ideas and form of this book to emerge and unfold naturally, bit by bit, I have been comfortable with myself and comfortable with the work.

It has not always been easy, by any means. There were moments, as there usually are in the creative process, when nausea set in, and I was tempted to chuck this project. But after rest and relaxation, new ideas would present themselves and spur me on to give them life and form.

In the process of writing, I have also often been simultaneously aware of the question that stimulated this book: the integral connection between creativity in the arts, sciences, and philosophy, and creativity in spirituality. They are distinct, but not separate. Spirituality flows into the other two realms of creativity, the affective and cognitive realms, and creativity in those realms flows out of spirituality. In this sense, creativity and spirituality are co-extensive.

Whatever our talents in the affective and cognitive realms, those talents are discovered, developed, and actualized through the living of our lives. Living our lives, in turn, is enriched and deepened through the creation of discrete artworks that grow out of our talents. Creativity and spirituality are one. We may isolate them for the sake of discussion, but we cannot isolate them in the reality of our lives.

Spirituality is consciously living an authentic life. Whether we are Buddhist, Christian, Jew, or atheist, the more consciously we live an authentic life, the more spiritual we are. We can, of course, live our life authentically without being conscious that we do.

Similarly, we can be creative without being aware of our creativity. I recall vividly a television interview with Kathryn Hepburn, one of my favorite actresses. Following some clips of exuberant scenes from her films, the interviewer asked Ms. Hepburn how she did what she did. With verve, and characteristically graceful hand gestures, she spontaneously replied, "Dah-ling, I don't *know* and I don't *care!*" It is one thing to be creative and another to be aware of one's creative process.

Earlier I defined creativity as the process of connecting that brings something new into being. This process is natural and nonrational, yet it is rationally controlled. Spirituality is an alternative specification of creativity. As such, it is a natural, nonrational process rationally controlled. Three elements distinguish spirituality from the affective and cognitive realms of creativity: the principal agent, the principal operation, and the outcome.

In making an artwork in the affective and cognitive realms, the artist or thinker is the primary agent and

God is the secondary agent. In affective creativity an artist *makes* something new. The poet makes a poem out of words; the painter makes a painting out of pigments; a sculptor makes a sculpture out of clay, or wood, or metal; a composer makes a symphony out of tones; a choreographer makes a dance out of movements. In cognitive creativity a philosophical thinker creates a new system of ideas, and a scientific thinker creates a new theory about the nature of physical reality. Thinkers *think* something new into being.

In spirituality, God is the principal agent and the human person is the secondary agent. On the natural levels of body and psyche, we grow and develop. On the level of spirit, God transforms us into a new creation. In making an artwork of our life, our principal activity is to live. God is the source and sustainer of our life. As we live out the connections between subjective reality, our interior life, and objective reality, our exterior life, a new person comes into being.

Creativity and spirituality complete and deepen one another. The processes and many elements in the process are similar. Similar attitudes and techniques and problems arise in both. As we work at the artworks that are given us, we can transfer much of what we learn to making an artwork of our own life. Similarly, as we work at the artwork of our own life, we can transfer attitudes and techniques learned in the process to the creation of discrete artworks in the other two realms.

Prevailing psychologies of creativity do not sufficiently take into account the domain of spiritual creativity. Such psychologies are limited to the affective and cognitive realms. In discussion of these two areas, psychologists sometimes refer to the saints and mystics as examples of the creative process. They do not clearly recognize the spiritual as a distinct realm.

For many years this blurring of the spiritual puzzled me. Over time, I began to see that it makes sense historically. Before the twentieth century, thinkers posited a duality of body and spirit. In the early twentieth century, with the emergence of depth psychology, thinkers posited a duality of body and psyche. With the work of Carl Jung and Otto Rank, the more likely truth began to emerge. Human beings are neither a duality of body and spirit nor a duality of body and psyche. We are, as Robert Doran puts it, a "compound in tension" of body, psyche, and spirit.

With the development of holistic depth psychology now taking place in the work of Ira Progoff and others, the reality of spirit and the interplay among body, psyche, and spirit are becoming clearer. The physical sciences, too, are becoming aware of the reality, nature, and workings of spirit in the universe. These studies hold much promise for the future of creativity and spirituality.

Distinctions   also are becoming clearer in philosophy. In the history of ideas, the "eternal verities" were beauty, truth, and goodness. In his book *The Idea of the Holy*, Rudolf Otto further clarifies the realm of the good. He distinguishes between the good and the holy. The good lies within the human compass. The human being is the principal agent in responsible conduct. But the holy transcends the good and includes the numinous. God is the principal agent in the creation of the holy.

I have come to sense that there may be still another distinction to be made in the realm of the holy. There is the experience of the holy, and there is the awareness of that experience. Saints are holy; mystics are aware of holiness.

Like other artists, many persons may live holy lives without being aware of what they are doing. They live the connections between interior reality and exterior reality. They live a spiritual life.

Mystics not only live holy lives, but they are also aware of holiness. They live the connections between subjective reality and objective reality. They experience God incarnate, and they also experience the connections between immanent reality and transcendent reality. They live the connections, and they are aware of doing so. They see God acting in their own lives and in the lives of others. I believe that this is the meaning of the beatitude, "Blessed are the pure of heart for they shall see God."

In an earlier attempt to work out an understanding of the similarities and differences in creativity and spirituality, I gradually developed a "Wheel of Creativity." This Wheel was a synthesis of the elements in the creative process and distinctions among those elements. Perhaps this is the place to include that Wheel . . . ?

Some years before that, I also developed a spherical model of human consciousness. Most models of human consciousness grew out of the sense that within the human person there are layers of depth and levels of consciousness. For example, Carl Jung discerned the depth layers of the personal unconscious and the collective unconscious. Bernard Lonergan developed a model of levels of human consciousness: sense experience, understanding, judgment, responsibility, and love.

The human person develops toward a wholeness imperfectly attained in this life. The person is transformed by the Spirit. On the analogy of the planets in space, I saw the sphere as a possible model of human consciousness. This sphere has spirit at both its center and its surface. Perhaps this is the place to insert that previous work as well . . . ? Somehow, the thought of doing so makes me uncomfortable. It is late. I will think about this tomorrow.

Against Pouring New Wine Into Old Skins

Morning: two funny things happened last night. I had spent a little time with some new acquaintances at the University Club. Then I watched a TV interview with Jesse Jackson. Since I did not feel tired, I wrote a little. Soon I found myself uncomfortable with the direction my writing was taking.

This morning I realized why. I could not include those models of human consciousness and creativity, because I am no longer the person who developed them. I have changed. Those models were syntheses of analyses. They were attempts to make things perfectly clear that are not in reality perfectly clear. They were attempts to contain creativity, if not in a box then in a sphere and a circle. They were attempts to contain what cannot be contained. They were static, and the nature of creativity is dynamic. That is why they resisted my including them here. They do not really belong here, and although I did not know that at first, they did.

Not that analysis of the creative process is inappropriate. Not that models of that process are inappropriate. Analyses and models may well be appropriate and helpful. But such models must be dynamic and organic. This past year, I developed a model of a creative process for writing an essay for my composition classes. This model, *Writing in Process: A Journey Toward an Essay* is organic. With it I tried to provide students with an analysis of the principal steps in the process of essay writing. It did seem to help many students. I still feel comfortable with that model. But the other two must go. They are no longer true for me.

Coming to Rest and Moving On

The second funny thing happened as I lay in bed letting my thoughts roam over yesterday's events and plans for resuming my work on *Connecting* this morning. Not one idea presented itself to me, yet neither did I feel blocked. I had no sense of how to proceed, nor did I feel inhibited in proceeding. I gradually became aware that I felt nothing at all. At the same time, I felt content and peaceful.

I have had such an experience before in other circumstances, but this time it puzzled me. Why did I feel this way? I have this work to finish, yet I felt neither the forward flow of the creative process nor a blockage in that process. I felt nothing.

Connection: the process and I had both come to rest. This meant that it was no doubt time to end this book. There was probably no more to be said, so I should say nothing. Simple. Just let it be and let it be as it is.

But I also realized that I have been in relation to you, *Connecting*, so I should not really make that decision without consulting you about it. So I decided that this morning I would do another dialogue with you, to see if you required anything further from me.

Dialogue with *Connecting*

Brief focusing statement: I sense that our work and play together is over and that it is time to let you go about your business while I move on to other things.

Stepping Stones in the History of Our Relationship:

- the idea to write you in 1980

- developing the model of human consciousness

- developing the Wheel of Creativity

- teaching the course in creativity

- writing *Journey toward an Essay*

- taking the course in spirituality

- finding myself with three weeks of "free" time

- puzzlement over where to go and what to do

- decision to remain at Notre Dame and write you

- discussion with a friend over my block in writing you

- breakthrough to how and why to proceed

- thirteen days of writing

- a sense of coming to rest and completion

- decision to consult you about concluding

Dialogue:

Me: Well ,*Connecting*, this is certainly an interesting development. As I began listing Stepping Stones above, I realized that I had not included such a list when I first dialogued with you many pages ago, as I should have done to get a sense of your history from your point of view. Secondly, after I listed the Stepping Stones, I noticed that they were not from your point of view, but from my own, on our growing relationship.

C.: That is interesting, Christian. But let it be. We both understand. Let us be about our dialogue.

Me: Okay, C. The thing I want to know is how you feel about our concluding our work at this point. I guess the relevant question is, "Do you feel ready to make your way alone into the world?"

C.: As I hear that question, C., I guess I do. I feel complete – at least for now. You have allowed me to come into being in my own way and time, and I appreciate that.

Me: But are you ready to do your own work now?

C.: I don't really know that, but I think I am. Why not let me go and try my wings? If I am not

ready, I will come to know that, and then we can
get back together again to see where we go from
there.

Me: That makes sense. Try it and see. If you need
further development or refinement, we can work
on that as the need arises.

C.: Makes sense to me. You aren't throwing me out
in the cold. You are giving me a chance to make
my own way, but under your watchful care.

Me: Yes. I will continue to nurture you if you need it.
If you are able to be completely independent of
me now, then you should be, and I will let you go.

C.: Thanks, C., I needed that.

Me: So did I.

C.: Now that that is settled, "What next?"

Me: Well, I was going to ask if you required anything
else of me, but I guess that the question has been
answered.

C.: Any other questions?

Me: Well, I also intended to ask you what you wanted
to be. But that question, too, has been answered.
You already are, and you are what you are. So be
it.

C.: So be it. Thanks for everything, C. I enjoyed it.

Me: Thank you, C. I enjoyed it, too. And I learned a great deal from you about creativity.

C.: What stands out for you now as we bring this stage of our relationship to a close?

Me: I have learned how really dynamic you are. You move, forward and back, breaking new ground and then returning over old ground to refine yourself, establish your direction, and find new direction.

C.: Just like your own life process.

Me: It seems so.

C.: Did you learn anything else of value?

Me: I learned how important it is to trust you, to trust that you know what is good for you better than I do. So I should trust that you will do what is best if I let you. My role is to help you to do that, not do it for you.

C.: I am grateful for that, C. You see, I do have a life and needs and destiny of my own, just as you do.

Me: I see that more clearly and deeply now. How often I have distorted and falsified you in the past.

C.:   No need to feel guilt over that. As you wrote, guilt is destructive; sorrow is creative.

Me: I really sense the distinction now. As my friend said, "I will know how sorry you are the next time." So, the next time I find you working in me, I will try to do better.

C.:   That's good. Be at peace in that.

Me: I feel that I am. I feel satisfied. It has been a great grace to have another chance at you, a chance to work more properly with you.

C.:   That adage that opportunity knocks but once is only partly true. You may miss an opportunity that knocks, or you may accept it badly. But often, if you are alert, you will be given another chance to do something similar and do it better second time around.

Me: That is encouraging.

C.:   Encouraging: from the root word for "heart." Take heart, Christian. Have courage and move forward. Move forward yourself and let me move forward.

Me: I will try. I realize that I am no longer so afraid of you.

C.:   Why do you think that is?

Me: I guess because I have seen that you are not out to get me, but to help make me.

C.: Very good, C. You are learning. I exist for your benefit, not your harm.

Me: And my benefit resides in letting you do your thing.

C.: Sure, because I am meant to do that, with or without your cooperation. If you don't cooperate, it is your loss as much as mine. If you do cooperate, we can make some contribution to the world, however large or small, and have fun doing it.

Me: And that contribution is for others to judge, not me.

C.: Right. You just do the best you can, no more, no less. Right?

Me: I think I am learning that.

C.: I think you are, too. And you are learning how important it is to be open.

Me: Yes. When I am open, I am alert to opportunities that present themselves to me, almost casually, as Dorothy Day recognized.

C.: That's how it happens. All organically, very simply, in the due course of living your life.

Me: Simply. I see, too, much more deeply how important it is to be simple. Just let things go their way. No big deal. No getting in the way with my trying to figure things out. They really cannot be figured out. They just work out.

C.:   That's it. They just work out if you don't interfere.

Me: So often I interfere.

C.:   Remember – no guilt. Just learn from your mistakes and try to do better next time. That is true repentance.

Me: And repentance is fertile. Genuine repentance makes us sensitive to new opportunities. Guilt closes us to them.

C.:   Right again, C. Guilt closes you up, hardens you. Genuine sorrow opens you up to new possibilities.

Me: New possibilities. We are offered so many, if we but recognize and accept them when they come.

C.:   Right again. You must accept the opportunities offered you, not try to manufacture your own. They are the real opportunities, the ones you can do something worthwhile with.

Me: But we do have to seek out opportunities, too. We don't just sit around waiting for opportunity to knock.

C.: No, you don't. The seeking out you are to do is to go about satisfying the needs and desires that you become aware of – your own and others. In doing that, you are available for real opportunities for service.

Me: Being available. That is a key, isn't it? We have to make ourselves available to serve needs and desires.

C.: Yes, because you see now that God incarnates God's needs and desires in individual human beings. When you respond as best you can to those needs and desires, you are responding to God.

Me: How little we know God, and how little we know ourselves.

C.: So true. But you learn and learn slowly. You learn that the better you know yourself and relate to yourself, the better you know God and relate to God in yourself and in every other human being.

Me: That seems to be at the heart of the matter, the real meaning of the truth that we are made in the image and likeness of God. If that is true – and I would stake my life on it – then it makes sense. God is in the deepest part of me. The better I know that deepest self and the more I allow that deepest self to live in me and through me, the better I know God and the more God is alive in the world.

C.:   Such a mystery, Christian. You cannot solve a mystery. You can only live it.

Me: More and more I accept that. I have spent so much time trying to solve what can only be lived, trying to contain what cannot be contained. God is life and love. Both are mysteries, and neither can be contained. They must be free to be as they are, become what they will become, and do what they will do.

C.:   Having done your part with me, you are free to move on, and I am ready. So let's do it. For God's sake, don't sit down!

Me: For God's sake, I'll try not to. Thanks, *Connecting*, for all you have taught me about yourself and about myself.

C.:   Thanks, Christian, for being willing to learn and live. God in peace and joy.

Me: You too, *Connecting*. Fare well. I love you.

C.:   Fare well, Christian. I love you, too.